DROID™
Companion

ERIC BUTOW
JOLI BALLEW

WILEY

John Wiley & Sons, Inc.

Droid™ Companion
Published by
John Wiley & Sons, Inc.
10475 Crosspoint Boulevard
Indianapolis, IN 46256
www.wiley.com

Copyright © 2012 by John Wiley & Sons, Inc. Indianapolis, Indiana

Published simultaneously in Canada

ISBN: 978-1-118-13168-8
ISBN: 978-1-118-22726-8 (ebk)
ISBN: 978-1-118-23217-0 (ebk)
ISBN: 978-1-118-23218-7 (ebk)

Manufactured in the United States of America

10 9 8 7 6 5 4 3 2 1 005.365 BUT

Library of Congress Control Number: 2011937923

Michelle, I'm taking your advice. Wherever you are,
I hope you're happy. You earned it.

Eric Butow

For my soon-to-be-born first grandchild; may your
life be filled with technological wonders I can't
even begin to imagine!

Joli Ballew

+ ABOUT THE AUTHORS

ERIC BUTOW is the owner of Butow Communications Group (BCG) in Jackson, California. BCG offers web development, online marketing, technical documentation, and computer-based training to small- and medium-sized businesses. He has written 18 books, with one translated into Chinese and another being revised for a second edition. One of those books is about the Samsung Galaxy Tab, a larger cousin of the Droid Charge. Eric has also developed and taught networking and usability courses for Ed2Go and California State University, Sacramento. When he's not working in (and on) his business or writing books, you can find Eric enjoying time with friends, walking around the historic Gold Rush town of Jackson, and helping his parents manage their infant and toddler daycare business.

JOLI BALLEW is a full-time author and technical writer. She has written more than 40 books for publishers worldwide, some of which have been translated into multiple languages. Joli has written books introducing all kinds of devices, including the BlackBerry Storm 2, the Motorola Xoom, and the iPad. When she isn't writing, Joli stays busy teaching at two local community colleges, Brookhaven Community College and Collin College, maintaining various websites, and managing the networks and their computers for a handful of local companies. Joli also attends various technical conventions to stay on top of the newest technologies. Last, but certainly not least, Joli is a mom, a soon-to-be grandma, a Microsoft MVP, and the butler for two cats and their gerbil, George.

+ ABOUT THE TECHNICAL EDITORS

JAMES TRUSCOTT (MCSE, MCPI, Network+) has extensive technical experience in many fields. James' passion for computers started back in the 1970s when he was a programmer for Bell Telephone. Over the years he has been a beta tester for many products, including new programs, VOIP telephones, and several hardware products including cell phones. In 2000, he taught MCSE classes at Eastfield College and the Dallas County Community College District; later he was the senior instructor for the Cowell Corporation teaching SBC employees how to employ remote access on encrypted laptops. He has served as webmaster for Cowell Corporation, and is currently a website contributor for the City of Garland, TX. James also does consulting work for several Dallas-based businesses. Over the years he has been the Technical Editor for many technical books and articles too, including the MCSE series from Syngress Books. In fact, James edited Joli Ballew's very first book, *Windows 2000 Professional*. At the current time, James is busy creating the next must-have iPhone app, and works for the City of Garland in various capacities.

TANIA VON ALLMEN began editing in college where, as the Teacher's Assistant for a BASIC computer-programming course, she did all the editing for the professor's soon-to-be-published textbook. It was here that she learned how to translate technical jargon into understandable language for the rest of us who may not have Ph.D.s in computer science. She graduated with a degree in Business Administration and has been using technology as an entrepreneur for the last 20 years to build her own small business. In true early adopter form she learned technology on the fly and jumped in fearlessly to discover the very kinds of things readers of this book want to know but might be afraid to try. She is the sort of person who will not hesitate to ask, "What does *this* button do?" Her love of gadgets inspired her to write a blog in 2010 called GadgetSister in which she reviewed new technology and lauded the features of her favorite electronic toys. Over the last several years, she has edited and illustrated a book of inspiring quotations, ghost written an autobiography, and is now currently finalizing a novel she will publish before the end of 2011. Tania lives with her family and works near Sacramento, California.

➕ CREDITS

Executive Editor
Robert Elliott

Senior Project Editor
Adaobi Obi Tulton

Technical Editors
James Truscott
Tania von Allmen

Production Editor
Kathleen Wisor

Copy Editor
Apostrophe Editing Services

Editorial Manager
Mary Beth Wakefield

Freelancer Editorial Manager
Rosemarie Graham

Associate Director of Marketing
David Mayhew

Marketing Manager
Ashley Zurcher

Business Manager
Amy Knies

Production Manager
Tim Tate

**Vice President and Executive
Group Publisher**
Richard Swadley

**Vice President and Executive
Publisher**
Neil Edde

Associate Publisher
Jim Minatel

Project Coordinator, Cover
Katie Crocker

Compositor
Maureen Forys,
Happenstance Type-O-Rama

Proofreader
Jen Larsen, Word One

Indexer
Johnna VanHoose Dinse

Cover Designer
Roger Gienger

Cover Image
© Denis Zbukarev

✛ ACKNOWLEDGMENTS

We wanted to get this book in your hands as quickly as possible, and under such tight deadlines you need as much help as you can get. Fortunately, I had plenty of it. Joli Ballew provided valuable guidance and feedback, and she's a very nice person, too. My support team at Wiley, executive editor Robert Elliott and project editor Adaobi Obi Tulton, kept me and Joli on track, and despite some health issues I've had, they never flagged in their encouragement. Copy editor San Dee Phillips of Apostrophe Editing Services tightened up our prose and cleaned up any grammar issues. And my technical editor, Tania von Allmen, lived up to her sterling reputation as GadgetSister.

My parents deserve special thanks for letting me write, especially when I couldn't help occupy the daycare kids (and you'll see a couple of pictures of them in this book). Finally, I want to thank my wonderful agent, Carole Jelen. It's no exaggeration when I say I wouldn't be where I am today without her.

Joli would like to thank everyone at Wiley, Eric her coauthor, her agent Neil Salkind, and her family. Everyone offers continual support and encouragement, and she is grateful for it.

✛ CONTENTS AT A GLANCE

✛ CONTENTS

✛ INTRODUCTION

Congratulations on your new Droid smartphone! You're going to be amazed when you discover all the ways it enables you to connect with your contacts and stay in touch with the world. You can communicate via talk, text, email, social networking, and chatting with instant messaging, and on some newer Droid phones, you may even be able to chat with live video through Google Talk. You can use the built-in cameras to take and share pictures and video, and the microphone to record audio; you can stream media to your phone from your home network (and back again). Even with all this, you're just scratching the surface!

The reason your Droid phone is special is two-fold. First, it runs a mobile operating system and offers built-in tools for browsing for and accessing data you store on it. In the past, you downloaded a third-party app for this, and managing data was more difficult. Second, it's high-tech: It's open to developers, and updates are also made available regularly. When you keep your phone updated, you keep your phone in tip-top shape too.

Beyond the technology though, you also have access to the Market, which enables you to easily browse, download, and install apps that do just about everything. And depending on your model, you can use your Droid phone to connect with others using various hardware. Your phone may have a HDMI out port, front and/or rear facing digital/video cameras, and a large enough screen with the display capabilities it needs to offer an impressive video-watching experience. To sum it up, it's cool.

You can enjoy your Droid phone for a long time, at least in tech-years. It offers you room to grow, and the more you learn about how to use the features it offers, the more you can begin to depend on it for tasks you never thought possible. Just wait until you send your first email by *saying* what you want in the body instead of *typing* it there! And the first time you experience playing a movie or some music on your Droid and streaming it to a compliant device on your home network, well, both you and your friends will be blown away!

With newer Droid phones, the problem of syncing has also been addressed. If you've ever had a phone and had no idea how to get music on it, you understand. If you've had to input your contacts manually, ditto. With new Droids, you can physically connect the device and sync using a program such as Windows Media Player, or you can opt to wirelessly copy the media through a compatible home network and compatible network devices. For contacts, you can upload those to the cloud (on Google's servers) and sync them over the air.

Whatever model you have and however you use it, you have a Droid phone of some sort, and it's awesome. It's different from what you're used to though, and you need a bit of instruction. This book focuses on four popular Droid phones: The Motorola Droid X2, the Motorola Droid 3, the Droid Incredible 2, and the Droid Charge. It doesn't matter if you have another model though, because all Droid phones run the Android operating system. They all access the Market the same way, through the Market icon. They all have Home screens; they all have a Menu button to access additional commands and settings; and they all offer some way to make calls, place texts, and get on the web.

This book takes you through the way you'll want to explore your phone. It starts with unpacking, getting you signed up with a Google Account, getting you connected to your own Wi-Fi network, walking you through the basic touch techniques so that you can get a feel for how the Droid works, and shows you how to personalize your Droid with data, backgrounds, apps, pictures, music, and movies. With that complete, you then learn how to make phone calls; obtain, listen to, watch, and share media; how to incorporate contacts and use calendars; and how to get the most out of your Droid at work and at play. The latter is included in a bonus chapter on our website at www.wiley.com/go/droidcompanion. We got so excited while writing this book we wrote too much for it to hold!

Enjoy!

CHAPTER ONE

HOW DO I GET STARTED WITH DROID?

To start with your Droid phone, you have to install the battery; activate it with your cellular service provider; familiarize yourself with the physical parts; join a Wi-Fi network; learn how to navigate the screens, menus, and other graphical parts; and learn a little about how to use the keyboard. After you're acquainted with the device and can move around successfully in it, you may want to connect a Bluetooth device and protect the Droid from unauthorized access.

Setting Up Your Droid Phone

If you purchased your new phone at a physical store, it's highly likely that the salesperson unboxed the phone, inserted the battery, turned it on, activated it, made a test call, and even guided you through inputting the required Google account. If that happened, you can skip forward to the "Exploring Google Apps and Services" section, stopping to read only the notes and such between here and there. If your new phone is still in the box and has not been activated, you need to continue here.

UNPACKING, CHARGING, AND GETTING READY

To start, carefully remove everything from the box. Lay the items out on a roomy table or desk, and take note of everything that's there. You have several pieces of material to read, including information about activation agreements and pricing plans, coverage areas, consumer information, safety and warranty information, and something along the lines of "how to master your device." The latter is important; it outlines how to insert the battery, attach the battery cover, and properly charge your phone. It may also tell you how to insert the microSD card, if applicable. The SIM should already be inserted.

Start by following the specific instructions for your device to insert the microSD card and battery, and attach the battery cover. If the directions tell you to charge the phone for a specific amount of time before using it, do so. While your phone is charging, read the rest of the information, specifically noting how to power on the device, what the external ports provide, and how to power off the device. Then, place the packaging back in the box, and keep the box handy. You may need to access the information later.

COMPLETING FIRST-TIME SETUP TASKS

When you first turn on your new Droid phone (by pressing and holding the Power button for a couple of seconds), you need to work through a few setup processes. Although tasks differ from device to device, they likely include the following:

+ Choosing a language

+ Activating the phone

+ Inputting your Google account information

+ Adding email accounts

+ Setting up some kind of "backup assistant"

+ Enabling phone location services from your carrier, from standard GPS, and Google location services

Follow these steps to set up the Droid X2 and the Droid 3 (and virtually any other Droid phone):

1. Turn on the phone and tap Select Language.

2. Select your language.

3. Tap the Android icon.

4. Tap Activate.

5. Tap Speaker, if wanted.

6. Follow the instructions to activate your phone, which involves the following:

    A. Tapping a specific key, perhaps 1.

    B. Tapping Next.

    C. Agreeing to the Terms of Service.

After the activation tasks are complete, you're ready to add your Google account. In the next section you learn how to get a Google account if you don't have one, and how to input that account using your phone.

CREATING AND INPUTTING A GOOGLE ACCOUNT

During the setup process, you are prompted to input a Google account and complete a few related setup tasks. You can skip the step that involves inputting a Google account and do it later if you want, but we suggest you take the time now. If you don't already have an account, when you get to step 4, tap Create, and follow the prompts to create an account. When it is created, you can continue with the directions to input that information to your Droid phone.

When prompted to input your Google account from your Motorola Droid X2, Droid 3, the Droid Incredible 2, and the Droid Charge, follow these steps:

1. If the screen has gone dark, press the Power button.

2. Tap Next.

3. Read the information offered, and tap Next again.

4. If you don't have an account, tap Create and follow the prompts. If you have an account, tap Sign In.

5. Input your Google Account username and password. If you use a virtual keyboard, tap Done.

6. Tap Sign In.

7. You'll be prompted that you can use your Google Account to back up your apps, settings, and other data. Tap Next to set this up.

8. Tap Finish Setup.

Finally, you'll be prompted to input a 4-to-8 digit PIN. Enter this, write it down, and keep it somewhere safe, and make any other configuration choices here. You can opt, for instance, to authorize Verizon to send your PIN to your phone if it's lost. Tap Submit to complete these tasks.

WHAT IF I WORK FOR A COMPANY THAT USES GOOGLE APPS FOR ENTERPRISE, AND I HAVE ONE OF THOSE ACCOUNTS? If your company uses Google Apps for Enterprise and you have a related account, you could use that account to set up your Droid phone. We warn against this. Instead, create a new Google account that's yours and yours alone. You can always add the Google Apps account as a second email account if you want to, but this way, if you change jobs, you'll still have your personal information through your personal Google account, and you can still use your Droid effectively.

CONFIGURING ADDITIONAL ACCOUNTS AND
ENABLING LOCATION SERVICES

As you can see in Figure 1-1, when you finish all the required setup tasks, you are prompted to configure any additional accounts you use. You might want to take this time to input your username and password for Facebook, Twitter, Photobucket, Google, Yahoo! Mail, and others. To input any of these, simply tap the icon and follow the prompts. If you have any difficulty using the keyboard (either physical or virtual), for now, refer to the information booklet that came with your phone. That tells you how to input an @ sign, _ character, uppercase letters, and so on. (There are also a few typing tips offered later in this chapter.) Tap Done Adding Accounts when finished. (If your screen goes dark, press the Power button, and move the Lock icon from left to right to unlock your phone.)

FIGURE 1-1 After setup, you have access to the Setup accounts screen.

Finally, you are prompted to enable various forms of location services. You can use location services to determine where you are currently positioned by using location data from cellular towers, Wi-Fi hotspots, or plain-old GPS. Actually, these can tell you where your *phone* is located, not you!

With your location information pinpointed, apps such as Maps can offer directions from your current location to another, inform you of transportation options in your area, and help you locate restaurants, coffee shops, bars, hotels, gas stations, and other places of interest. Third party apps may offer even more information, let you "check in" to establishments you frequent, tell others where you are via social networking, and more. It's up to you to enable location services. Some people feel it's an invasion of privacy; others, like us, look at it as just another useful service to help apps work better and our phones perform more effectively. You'll be prompted by new apps, as you obtain them, to let them have access to your location, and you can generally opt to allow or disallow the first time you open the app. When you see a Home screen like the one shown in Figure 1-2, setup is complete.

FIGURE 1-2 When you see the Home screen, your phone is ready to use.

Using External Controls

Your Droid phone is composed of physical hardware. Many components are housed inside the device, including things such as video camera hardware, internal memory, Bluetooth and wireless hardware, and the processor. Your Droid has hardware available to you on the outside of the device, too.

EXPLORING WHAT'S AVAILABLE ON ALL PHONES

The external hardware that is unique to your phone is called out in the documentation that came with it, and you should take a look at that documentation now. However, you absolutely must be familiar with a few pieces of hardware, so if you can't get your hands on the original documentation at the present time, you can use the list here to locate controls you immediately need. You may have to look carefully and closely to locate these items, but you should find them.

These hardware features are available on all Droid phones:

+ **Power/Lock key**—This button is normally located on the top of the phone. To power on or off, hold for 2–3 seconds. To lock or unlock, simply press quickly once. The Power button is nearly always one finger width in size. You can't cause any harm to the phone by pressing these buttons, although you may find the screen goes dark if you press the Power/Lock key.

+ **Volume**—Volume controls on both the Incredible 2 and the Droid Charge are on the left side when the phone is held in Portrait mode. On the Droid X2 and the Droid 3 they are on the right side. Press the top button to increase volume and the bottom one to lower it. A Volume icon appears on the screen when you do this, as shown in Figure 1-3. You can also use these keys to zoom where applicable. The Volume controls are two finger widths in size.

LOCATING VIDEOS ON THE WEB If you're having trouble locating the external controls on your phone, and you can't find the user's guide that came with it, check out the information available on the web. At www.verizon.com for instance, you can access the "Wireless" section of the website, tap Support for Your Device, and look up the support pages for your phone. Many of the phones have a "interactive how-to simulator" section, which offers videos for how to do things, like turning the device on or off or working through the setup wizards.

FIGURE 1-3 A volume graphic appears on the screen when you increase or decrease the volume.

✦ **Headphone jack**—The headphone jack is generally located at the top of the device.

✦ **Camera lens**—You can find the camera lens on the back of the phone. You use it to take still pictures and videos.

✦ **HDMI Port**—The HDMI Port is generally located at the bottom-left or bottom-right corner of the phone if you're holding the phone in portrait mode. Use this to connect your Droid to a compatible HDMI device, such as a television or projector.

✦ **Mini USB Port**—The mini USB port is generally located on the bottom-left or bottom-right corner, again when in portrait mode, of the phone and is often just above the HDMI port. It's a small port that you use to connect the Droid to the USB cable that comes with it, for the purpose of connecting to a computer or charger. You can also connect and use additional compatible devices.

✦ **Microphone**—Generally located near where you'd speak while on a phone call, the microphone is often recognizable by a small circular dot on the phone, near the bottom.

✦ **MicroSD Card Slot and SIM Tray**—The MicroSD card slot and SIM tray are located inside the device. Some Droid phones come with a microSD card already installed; others provide a slot, but the card is sold separately. SIMs are usually preinstalled.

✦ **Soft or hard buttons**—Generally, Droid phones have four buttons that run across the bottom of the screen. They can be hard buttons you physically push down, or soft buttons you tap. Often, with soft buttons, you feel a little vibration after pressing them. These buttons are often used to access menus (you might see four squares to denote this), to return to the default Home screen (you see an icon that looks like a house), to go back to a previous screen (represented by a backward arrow or U-turn arrow), and to perform a search (represented by a magnifying glass). Look at the icons that run across the bottom of your phone to see if you can make out what they do by looking at their icons.

WHAT EXACTLY IS A SIM CARD? SIM stands for Subscriber Identity Module. A SIM card identifies your device to a cellular data provider and includes information about your username, phone number, and other data as applicable.

FINDING WHAT'S UNIQUE TO YOUR PHONE

The best way to find out what's unique to your phone's hardware is to locate the external controls outlined in the previous section and see if there is any other hardware not yet accounted for. You may have a slide-out keyboard, for instance. Phones that become available after this book is published may include easily accessible microSD card readers. You may also determine from where sound comes (speakers).

Beyond what's unique to your phone is the external equipment you can purchase. You might want to buy a second phone charger, a charging dock, a Bluetooth headset, or conversion kits for using your phone overseas. You have to learn how to connect those devices, which devices are compatible, and how to use them.

That said, it's best to read the documentation that came with your phone now, especially if there are any external controls you see that you can't define. You can also visit the manufacturer's website to look for any must-have hardware. You'll find all kinds of information. For instance, almost all offer video tutorials for performing tasks, including how to do what we'll show in the next section on flicking, swiping, tapping, and the like.

CHECK FOR SYSTEM UPDATES Occasionally, the software that runs in the background to power your phone is updated. You can check for updates manually. Now is a good time to do that, before going much further into the book.

To check for updates on a Motorola Droid X2, Droid 3, or a Droid Charge phone, follow these steps:

1. Press the Menu button. This is the hard or soft button with the four squares on it.

2. Tap Settings.

3. Scroll down and touch About Phone.

4. Tap System updates.

5. If an update is available, install it.

To check for updates on a Droid Incredible 2, follow these steps:

1. Press the Menu button, which is the soft button with the three lines on it.

2. Tap Settings.

3. Scroll down and touch Software Update.

4. Tap Check New.

5. If an update is available, install it.

SWIPING, FLICKING, PINCHING, AND OTHER TOUCH TECHNIQUES

You use touch techniques to navigate the Droid's Home screens and its apps and menus. You also use touch techniques to surf the web with the browser, to type on a virtual keyboard (if applicable), to place calls, and more. You can learn techniques specific to apps as you work through this book. You need to know the basic techniques to start though, and following are a few of the techniques you can immediately apply:

- ✚ You *tap* once to open an app, choose an icon, or apply an option.

- ✚ You *tap, hold,* and *drag* an icon to move it. You can drag an icon to another area of the screen, to another screen, or onto the top of a folder you've created to group apps in. You can also tap and drag some widgets to resize them. You learn other uses for tapping and dragging as you work through this book.

- ✚ A *flick,* also called a *swipe,* is a quick motion in which you move your finger quickly from left to right, right to left, bottom to top, or top to bottom. Use this gesture to move from one Home screen to another; to move among pages in an eBook; to move from one picture to another in a picture app; to scroll through a long web page; and more.

- ✚ You can *pinch* to zoom in or out of a photo, map, or web page, among other things.

If you haven't done so yet, use a flicking technique to view the other Home screens on your phone:

1. If the screen is dark, press the Power button.

2. On most Droid phones, you place your finger on the Lock icon and slide right. On the Droid Incredible 2, you place your finger on the Lock icon and slide down.

3. Note what icons are on your Home screen.

4. Use your finger to tap and drag (flick) left. Repeat.

5. Use your finger to flick right. Repeat.

6. To verify you're on the default Home screen, press the physical Home button on your phone. (It has a picture of a house on it.) It's at the bottom.

ROTATING, FLIPPING, AND TWISTING

Beyond what you can do with a single finger, you can physically reposition your Droid to change the view. You can rotate it 90 degrees in any direction to change the view from portrait to landscape and back. Almost all the figures in this chapter are in Portrait view. Figure 1-4 shows Landscape view. Landscape view is often a more effective view to work in, because text seems to be easier to read, and if you have a model with a slide-out keyboard, it's readily available.

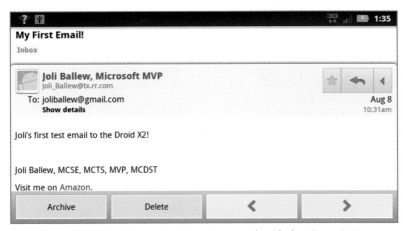

FIGURE 1-4 Often, Landscape view is easier to work with than Portrait view.

As long as you hold on tightly to it, you can flip the Droid so that it faces away from you. This automatically positions it so the person sitting across from you can see what you've been looking at. Of course, you can rotate the Droid 180 degrees, too. Flipping is great when you want to share a picture with a person across the table from you.

Finally, you can twist the Droid. Twisting is often used when you play a game. You might twist the Droid while playing a driving game to make a sharp turn, or twist to make a ball fall in a hole in a labyrinth game. The accelerometer makes this possible.

Browsing the Home Screen

The Home screen is the screen that appears when you turn on your Droid phone. Because you can flick left and right to access more Home screens, we refer to the one that appears when you turn on the phone as the "default" Home screen. Figures 1-2 and 1-3 showed examples of the default Home screen on the Droid 3 and the Droid X2. Figure 1-5 shows the default Home screen on the Droid Charge.

FIGURE 1-5 The Droid's Home screens are all similar.

Below the Home screen, not shown in Figure 1-5, located on the phone, are the hard and soft buttons detailed earlier. Use those to get to the default Home screen, go back, search for something, and access various menus. If you haven't yet experimented with those, do so now.

THE TOUCH SCREEN The screen is often referred to as the *touch screen* because you can touch it to interact with it. And, some items that appear across the bottom of the default Home screen appear on all of them. You can see those static icons when you flick left and right. It's likely that those static icons offer quick access to the phone, text messaging, the camera, and the All Apps window. These are often features and tools you need to quickly access. As with anything else though, you can personalize this to suit your needs. (See Chapter 2, "How Do I Make the Droid Uniquely Mine?")

EXPLORING SHORTCUTS, APPS, AND WIDGETS

On any Droid screen you may have access to various apps, shortcuts to apps, and widgets. These are all different things.

Apps are the actual applications that open when you tap their shortcuts. Apps are generally simple programs that you manipulate by tapping various parts in it. For instance, you can use the Calculator app to perform calculations, or the Gallery app to view photos. You can use the Browser app to surf the Internet. Apps can be games, productivity applications, e-book readers, and so on.

Some apps are quite impressive; the Voice Commands app enables you to speak a command, such as "Open Gmail," and Gmail opens. Maps is an app and is also quite comprehensive, offering directions, the ability to post reviews of places you visit, and an easy way to communicate with others who use similar applications and devices. There are others, which you will learn about throughout this book and as you explore your device.

A *shortcut to an app* is simply a graphic; you tap it once, and the related app opens. You can create your own shortcuts to apps you use most and place those shortcuts on any Home screen. You learn how to do this in the next chapter.

Widgets are extensions of apps; they offer a way to access quickly changing information without having to open any app. If you do decide you want more information, you can tap the widget to open it. Figure 1-6 shows two widgets we added: the Market widget and the News and Weather widget. The items shown in the widget change every few seconds.

To become familiar with widgets, add the News and Weather widget. On a Motorola Droid X2, Droid Charge, or Droid 3 (and you learn a lot more about this in Chapter 2), follow these steps:

1. Flick to an empty Home screen.

2. Press the Menu button on the phone. It's the button with the four squares.

3. Tap Add. (The order of the commands differs depending on the phone, but Add is an option on all phones.) See Figure 1-7.

4. Tap Android Widgets.

FIGURE 1-6 Widgets offer frequently changing data, such as the news and weather or the most popular apps from the Market.

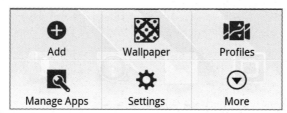

FIGURE 1-7 Add widgets to interact with your phone in new ways.

5. Tap News & Weather; tap News and Weather on the next screen.

6. Note the new widget.

7. If you'd like to explore further, tap the widget.

8. Tap the Menu button and tap Settings.

9. Review the settings and make changes as wanted.

The Droid Incredible 2 comes with separate News and Weather widgets. To add the News and Weather widgets to an Incredible 2:

1. Scroll to an empty Home screen.

2. Tap the Personalize button.

3. Tap Widget.

4. Tap News. The News widget appears.

5. Tap Select.

6. Tap Mobile Device.

7. Tap HTC – Latest in Support.

8. Tap Select. The newsfeed appears in the Home screen as shown in Figure 1-8.

9. Tap the Personalize button.

10. Tap Widget.

11. Tap Weather.

12. Tap Select. The weather widget appears on the Home screen as shown in Figure 1-9.

FIGURE 1-8 The newsfeed widget appears in the Home screen.

FIGURE 1-9 The weather widget appears in the home screen.

There are also two widgets for news and weather on the Droid Charge. They're called Daily Briefing News and Daily Briefing Weather. To add both widgets, follow these steps:

1. Flick to an empty Home screen.

2. Press the Menu button on the phone.

3. Tap Add.

4. Tap Widgets.

5. Tap Daily Briefing News. The AP Mobile news widget appears on the Home screen.

6. Press the Menu button.

7. Tap Add, and then tap Widgets.

8. Tap Daily Briefing Weather. The AccuWeather.com widget appears below the Daily Briefing News widget and asks you to tap the widget to get weather information for a specific city, as shown in Figure 1-10.

FIGURE 1-10 The AP Mobile news and Accuweather.com widgets on the Home screen.

BE CAREFUL WITH WIDGETS Certain widgets may run all the time, in the background, to offer you up-to-date information about the weather, breaking news, sports scores, stock prices, email, messages, and the like. When a widget obtains its updates or when updates are sent to it, data is transmitted. If you're away from a Wi-Fi network, it can get those updates through your data network. This can deduct data from the quota you have with your cellular data provider. Additionally, running widgets use more battery power than apps that run only when you need them. If you're concerned about battery life and data usage, limit widget use. Finally, widgets can be buggy. Make sure to read the reviews of widgets before putting them on your phone.

EXPLORING YOUR DROID'S STATUS BAR

The Status bar runs across the top of the screen and offers information about the type of network you're connected to, how strong that network is, and offers the current time, among other things. The Status bar is always present, no matter what Home screen you're on, what app you're using, or what widget you've opened.

The only other thing you need to know right now about the Status bar is that you can tap and drag (or pull down on) the Status bar to see additional notifications, as shown in Figure 1-11. The notifications may be about available Wi-Fi networks, as shown here, or they may tell you about the status of the phone, offer information about new messages you've received, and so on. Although there's not much to see in this figure, you can see that we're pulling down on the Status bar and that there are notifications available.

FIGURE 1-11 Tap the Status bar, hold your finger there, and then pull down on the Status bar to see notifications and ongoing activities, among other things.

Using the Menu Button

We've talked about the Menu button a few times in this chapter. This is the physical button on your phone that has four squares on it and is located near the bottom of your phone when held in Portrait view. However, you probably aren't aware of just how powerful it is. What you have access to when you press this button depends solely on what's open when you press it. When you press the Menu button while on a Home screen for instance, you can make changes to the Home screen; you can add widgets if you like or even change the wallpaper. However, pressing the Menu button causes different options to appear if you press it while using an app or while the All Apps page is open.

Whatever is available, when a set of options appear, you simply tap to make a choice. Most of the time you don't need to tap a setting and then tap Save or Apply like you would on a computer though; most of the time simply tapping an option applies it.

You already know what options appear when you press the Menu button when you are on a Home screen. To see how the Menu button appears in a different scenario on the Motorola Droid X2 or the Droid 3, follow these steps:

1. Tap the Open Apps icon on the screen. It's shown in Figure 1-12 as it appears on the Droid X2 and the Droid 3 and is square. On other Droid models it may appear as a 4 x 4 square icon, or it may appear as a box with four squares in it, detailed later.

2. To see all the items available on this page, flick left or right, or flick up or down, as applicable to your device. Use the drop-down arrow to choose All Apps if all of the apps aren't showing.

FIGURE 1-12
The Open Apps icon is square and is likely on your default Home screen.

3. Make sure no app is selected, and press the Menu button.

4. Note the options. Tap Sort Group on the Droid 3 and Sort on the Droid X2 and see what happens, as shown in Figure 1-13.

FIGURE 1-13 The Menu options change depending on what's open when you press the button.

5. Press the Back button on the phone.

6. Press the Menu button again. Press Search.

7. Type Gmail.

8. To open the Gmail app, tap it in the results.

To see what happens when you press the Menu button when an app is open on the Droid X2 or Droid 3, follow these steps:

1. Open Browser. This icon should be on one of the Home screens.

2. Press the Menu button.

3. Tap Bookmarks. See Figure 1-14.

FIGURE 1-14 When in an app, the Menu options change to reflect what options are available for it.

4. Note the available bookmarks already created.

5. Press the Back button, and press the Menu button again.

6. This time, tap New Window.

7. Press the Menu button and tap Windows.

8. Note the two windows you now have available. You can easily switch between them, or open more.

To see how the Menu button appears in a different scenario on the Motorola Droid Incredible 2, follow these steps:

1. Tap the Open Apps icon in the lower-left corner of the screen. It's shown in Figure 1-15 and has a four-by-four grid of squares (or 16 small squares, whatever you prefer).

2. To see all the items available on this page, flick up or down.

3. Make sure no app is selected, and press the Menu button.

4. Note the options. Tap Sort to see the options.

5. Press the Back button on the phone.

6. Tap List.

7. The apps appear in list form, as shown in Figure 1-16.

FIGURE 1-15 The Open Apps icon has a four-by-four grid of squares and is likely on your default Home screen.

FIGURE 1-16 The apps are in list form.

To see what happens when you press the Menu button when an app is open on the Droid Incredible 2, follow these steps:

1. Open Internet. This icon should be on one of the Home screens.

2. Press the Menu button.

3. Tap Bookmarks, as shown in Figure 1-17.

4. Note the available, already created bookmarks.

5. Press the Back button, and press the Menu button again.

6. This time, tap Windows.

FIGURE 1-17 When in an app, the Menu options change to reflect what options are available for it.

7. Tap the plus button at the upper-left corner of the screen just below the URL box.

8. Note the two windows you now have available. You can easily switch between them or open more.

To see how the Menu button appears in a different scenario on the Droid Charge, follow these steps:

1. Tap the Open Apps icon in the lower-right corner of the screen. It's shown in Figure 1-18 and has four squares.

2. To see all the items available on this page, flick left or right.

3. Make sure no app is selected, and press the Menu button.

4. Note the options. Tap Edit.

5. The apps appear with squares around them, as shown in Figure 1-19. You can rearrange the apps on the screen by holding the icon and then dragging it to its new location.

6. Press the Menu button. You can save or cancel your changes.

FIGURE 1-18 The Open Apps icon has four squares and is likely on your default Home screen.

FIGURE 1-19 The apps in edit mode.

To see what happens when you press the Menu button when an app is open on the Droid Charge, follow these steps:

1. Open Browser. This icon should be on one of the Home screens.

2. Press the Menu button.

3. Press New Window, as shown in Figure 1-20.

4. Note that you have created a new Browser window.

5. Press the Menu button again.

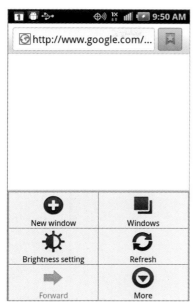

FIGURE 1-20 When in an app, the Menu options change to reflect what options are available for it.

6. This time, tap Windows.

7. See the two windows you now have available. You can easily switch between them or open more.

Exploring Google Apps and Services

Now that you know a bit about the external controls, the status icons, the touch screen, flicking and swiping, and how to move among Home screens, take a moment now look at some of the available Google Services on your phone. Browser, Market, Gmail, and others you'll read about here are all Google-based, and you'll find many of them on your Home screen, shown in Figure 1-21.

Following are a few of the Google apps you can find on your new Droid phone:

- **Calendar**—A free calendar you can use to create events and reminders. Calendar enables you to create and manage multiple calendars as well. Chapter 11 ("How Do I Use the Droid to Communicate and Work More Efficiently?") covers the Calendar app.

- **Gmail**—A free web-based email service. You can get email on your Droid phone through the Gmail app, or you can access your mail from any Internet-enabled device from `https://mail.google.com`. Chapter 6 ("How Do I Get the Most from the Messaging and Email?") explains the Gmail app.

FIGURE 1-21 All Droid phones offer similar Droid-only icons, like the Market and Browser.

- **Maps**—A free mapping service that can easily determine where you are and offer information and routes to get other places. Figure 1-22 shows the Maps app. Maps is detailed in Chapter 11.

- **Talk**—A free communication tool that enables you to send and receive instant messages and hold video chats, if your phone supports it. Your phone must run Android 2.3.4 or higher and meet other requirements before you can video chat. Chapter 6 explains the Talk app. (To find out the Android version on your phone, tap the Menu button, tap Settings, scroll down if necessary, and tap About Phone.)

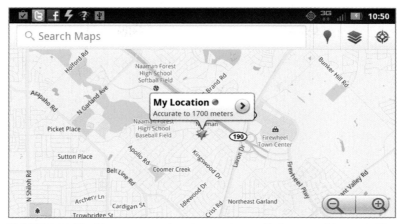

FIGURE 1-22 The Maps app uses location services to find your position and offers information about what's nearby.

✦ **YouTube**—A free video-sharing site. If your Droid phone supports it, you can upload your own video, like and dislike a video, flag a video, view related videos, post comments, and more. Your Google account is your YouTube account, should you be prompted. Chapter 10 ("How do I Best Take, View, Share, and Play Music and Video?") covers YouTube.

You learn more about the Google and Droid apps as you go along, although you probably already have a good idea of what to expect from each. However, with a configured Google account, you can explore the Google apps and services available on your Droid right now. You may be prompted to sign in to these apps the first time you use them (or agree to Terms of Service), but that's easy enough. If you'd like, tap the Market icon now, accept the Terms of Service, and take a look at the Market's interface. This can give you an idea of how to use your new phone; you tap an icon, and gain access to what it offers. (You can press the Home icon on the phone toward the bottom to return to the original Home screen.)

- -

THERE ARE MANY MORE GOOGLE APPS! Many more Google apps are available than what has been listed here, such as Google Docs, Google Sites, and Google Earth. To see what's available, visit `www.google.com/options`.

- -

JUST THE FACTS In the next section you learn only what you need to know to connect to a personal or business Wi-Fi network. You need to learn to connect to a Wi-Fi network as soon as possible, to limit your cellular data usage. When you connect to Wi-Fi, the data you use to surf, view videos, and perform other online tasks isn't counted against your usage counters with your cellular data provider. What's detailed here is the *least you need to know*. All of Chapter 4 ("How Do I Use and Manage the Wireless and Cellular Features?") is dedicated to wireless and cellular features and how to use them.

Connecting to a Personal or Business Wi-Fi Network

If you have a Wi-Fi network at home or in your favorite coffee shop, library, or pub, you're probably ready to connect to it so that you can stop relying on your cellular provider for Internet access. Wi-Fi is often faster than cellular, but you may have only a limited amount of data you can use, and you certainly don't want to go over your data limit.

TURN ON WI-FI Wi-Fi should be enabled out-of-the-box. If, for whatever reason, Wi-Fi is disabled or you can't see known wireless networks, you can enable it easily by following these steps:

1. Press the Menu button.
2. Tap Settings.
3. Tap Wireless & Networks.
4. Tap Wi-Fi.

The first step is to get within range of a Wi-Fi network that you believe you have permission to access. When there, pull down on the Status bar to see if there's a notification that a network is available. In Figure 1-23 on our Droid X2, one is available.

If you see a notification that a network is available on your Motorola Droid phone, follow these steps:

1. Tap Wi-Fi Networks Are Available.

2. Read the information offered, and tap OK.

3. Tap the network to connect to. See Figure 1-24.

FIGURE 1-23 The Status bar offers information about available Wi-Fi networks.

FIGURE 1-24 You may see multiple networks when you opt to connect.

4. Type the password, passcode, or passphrase.

5. If you use a virtual keyboard, tap Done.

6. Tap Connect.

7. When you see Connected, you're connected to the network.

8. Press the Home button to return to the Home screen.

9. Notice the new icon on the Status bar. It looks like an upside-down triangle.

If you know you should see a network but one isn't available, press the Menu button, tap Settings, and Wireless & Networks, shown in Figure 1-25. Tap Wi-Fi and select the network from there. Note that *only* in a Droid Charge, you need to pull down on the Status bar and tap the Wi-Fi icon to connect to a network.

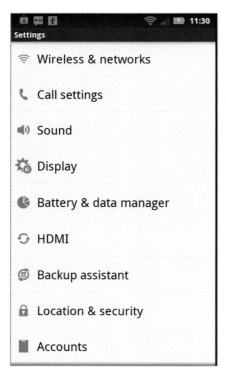

FIGURE 1-25 Tap Wireless & Networks to select a network.

LEAVE WI-FI ENABLED It's possible to turn off the wireless features of your phone. You'll learn how to do that in Chapter 4. (Although you can probably figure it out now.) People often do this to extend battery life. (And you must do it while on a plane.) However, if you leave Wi-Fi on, and you leave the setting Notify Me When an Open Network Is Available selected, you can really cut down on your data usage. That's because you'll be notified when free Wi-Fi networks are available, and you can join them. Additionally, after you connect one time, you'll be connected automatically the next time you're within range.

As an added bonus, Wi-Fi is generally faster than any cellular data option you have, be it 3G or 4G. And speaking of cellular data, when you connect to the Internet through a Wi-Fi network, you don't use any cellular data. This means if you have a limited data plan, that plan will last a little longer.

Of course, if you are in a situation in which you must preserve battery power, disable Wi-Fi. For more information refer to Chapter 4.

USE THE KEYBOARD You may not have used the virtual keyboard yet, or at least not much. If you have to use it to input credentials to join a Wi-Fi network, following are a few tips to help you along.

+ Tap a key to type a letter.
+ Tap the up arrow first if you need to uppercase a letter.
+ Tap the ⌫ to erase the last typed letter.
+ Tap the **.?123** key to access numbers and special keys. Tap **ABC** to return to the basic keyboard.
+ Use the spacebar to add a space.
+ Tap Done to hide the keyboard when finished with it.

Understanding Network Icons

The Status bar that runs across the top of your screen shows the Droid's Status icons, many of which you already explored (see Figure 1-26). One of the most important Status icons to understand is the Network icon. If you see an upside-down triangle, it means you're connected to a Wi-Fi network. You learned how to locate and connect to a Wi-Fi network in the previous section. If there's no Wi-Fi network available, and if you've signed up for cellular service through Verizon, On other Droid devices like the Xoom you can disable cellular service, I don't see that option on these phones. when you're away from a Wi-Fi network, your cellular data network will automatically be enabled and will take over the job to obtain Internet access.

If you don't see the Wi-Fi icon on the status bar, but instead see 3G, 4G, 1X, 2X, or some other icon, it means you're connected to Verizon's cellular network. This is important to note because you have to pay for cellular data service, and you want to keep your use to a minimum. If you go over your limit, you'll be charged extra. You may also see that no

FIGURE 1-26 The Status icon you should be looking for now is the Wi-Fi icon.

network is available if you are in an area where the Verizon cellular network is not available. In that case, your best option is to purchase a wireless adapter for another device such as a desktop or laptop computer and create a wireless hotspot that your Droid can access.

Connecting a Bluetooth Device

Bluetooth is a short-range (generally less than 30 feet) wireless technology that you can use to connect your Droid to Bluetooth hardware such as hands-free headsets, car kits, and other wireless devices. If you've purchased any of these devices, read on. Otherwise, you can skip this section. Before you start though, read any documentation that came with your Bluetooth device. Follow those if they differ from what's outlined here.

As with other wireless features, you can access the Settings app to start. If you recall, from any Home screen, you can press the Menu button and tap Settings to start. On the Droid X2, Droid 3, and Droid Incredible 2, here's what you do:

1. If applicable, turn on the Bluetooth device and make it discoverable.

2. On the Droid, press the Menu button.

3. Tap Settings.

4. Tap Wireless & Networks.

5. Tap Bluetooth (Turn on Bluetooth). See Figure 1-27.

FIGURE 1-27 Turn on Bluetooth to scan for devices.

6. Tap Bluetooth Settings.

7. Tap Discoverable, and then tap Scan for Devices.

8. If necessary, touch OK or enter the device passkey (such as **0000**). Often, the generic bluetooth code is 0000.

9. When the device is connected, you see the Bluetooth indication in the Status bar.

On the Droid Charge, here's how you start:

1. If applicable, turn on the Bluetooth device and make it discoverable.

2. On the Droid, press the Menu button.

3. Tap Settings.

4. Tap Wireless & Network.

5. Tap Bluetooth Settings.

6. Tap Bluetooth (Turn on Bluetooth). See Figure 1-28.

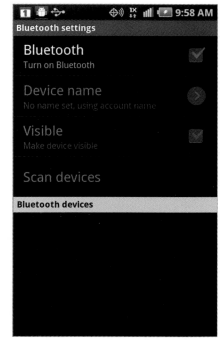

FIGURE 1-28 Turn on Bluetooth to scan for devices.

7. Tap Bluetooth Settings.

8. Tap Scan Devices if your Droid doesn't find any Bluetooth devices.

9. If necessary, touch OK or enter the device passkey (such as **0000**).

10. When the device is connected, you see the Bluetooth indication in the status bar.

SHOULD I JUST LEAVE BLUETOOTH ENABLED ALL THE TIME?
You might think it would be okay to leave Bluetooth enabled all the time because we encouraged you to leave Wi-Fi on all the time earlier in this chapter. However, this isn't the case. You just won't use Bluetooth that often, and there's no need to let it drain the battery when you don't need it. Just turn on Bluetooth when you need it, and turn it off when you don't.

Protecting the Droid from Unauthorized Access

Unless you configure some protections and take some precautions, anyone who gains access to your Droid can use it. If it's lost or stolen, whoever finds it can simply press the Power/Lock button, move the slider to unlock the screen, and have free rein to your personal data. If your kids get ahold of it, they can access anything they like as well, including email, apps, music, and video. Worse, they can use up your entire data plan watching YouTube videos, send email as you, or update your Facebook status. It's best to protect your Droid using the security features available.

ENABLING SECURITY AND SETTING A SCREEN LOCK

Several options are available to protect your Droid from unauthorized access, and they all require you to input something unique such as a pattern or credential for unlocking the screen. Following are several choices:

+ **None**—Never lock the screen. With this option, you press the Power/Lock button, move the slider, and the Droid's screen appears. This does not require a pattern, PIN, or password to unlock the screen. This offers no protection from unauthorized access. This is the default.

✚ **Pattern**—With this option, you can create your own unique pattern to unlock the screen. After a pattern is established, you unlock the Droid by dragging your finger across the screen in that way. You may opt to draw a letter on the screen, such as a Z, to unlock the screen, for instance. See Figure 1-29.

✚ **PIN**—Requires a numeric PIN to unlock the screen.

✚ **Password**—Requires a password to unlock the screen.

To configure any of these options, do this:

1. Press the Menu button and tap Settings.

2. Tap Location & Security.

3. Tap Set Up Screen Lock.

4. Select Pattern, PIN, or Password.

5. Enter the required information.

6. State how long to wait before the credential is required to unlock the screen after the screen has darkened on its own. (If you lock the screen by pressing the Power/Lock button, the Timeout period doesn't apply.)

   A. Tap Set Lock Timer.

   B. Select the wanted time period.

7. Press the Home button.

FIGURE 1-29 A pattern is a unique way to protect your new Droid phone.

USING ALTERNATIVE SECURITY OPTIONS

You may encrypt your accounts, settings, apps and related data, media, and other files stored on your Droid phone. When data is encrypted it's much harder for a thief or hacker to get to it. If you want to encrypt your Droid, go to Settings ⇨ Location & Security ⇨ Data Encryption to start.

You might also want to consider third-party apps. There are some that enable you to wipe the data from your Droid remotely, should it be lost or stolen. Mobile Defense is one of these apps. Various mobile security programs are also available from companies such as Norton and AVG. Because it's better to be safe than sorry, the next time you're in the Market app, search for Security. Review what's available and decide what's best for you and your phone.

- -

DISABLE VISIBLE PASSWORDS When you type a password, you may notice that the letters you type for the password show as you type them. Someone serious about snooping out your passwords may view what you type and steal those passwords. You can opt not to show passwords as you type them from the Settings app under Location & Security. (Someone can still watch you type the password though, so be vigilant.)

- -

Related Questions

- ✚ How can I personalize my Home screens? **PAGE 36**
- ✚ How do I get my personal data on my Droid? **PAGE 51**
- ✚ Where can I learn more about networks? **PAGE 100**
- ✚ How do I connect to my company's secure VPN? **ONLINE AT** www.wiley.com/go/droidcompanion

CHAPTER TWO

HOW DO I MAKE THE DROID UNIQUELY MINE?

In This Chapter:

+ Customizing the Screen

+ Getting Personal Data on Your Phone

The easiest way to make your Droid uniquely yours is to customize the screens with wallpaper, configure the placement and groupings of apps and widgets, and fill your Droid with personal data. After you read this chapter, your Droid (and ours) will no longer look the same. However, the Menu, Home, Back, and Search buttons will still be available, and the Status bar and Home screens will, too, so you can still find your way around. That said, feel free to add what you want and to make as many changes as you like!

Customizing the Screen

You can move around the widgets and apps on a single screen, move them to different screens, change the wallpaper that's shown on your screens, and even easily add or delete widgets from screens. You can also change any of the four icons on the Dock, the row of apps that appears at the bottom of the touch screen no matter what Home screen you're on. You can make these changes in various places on the Droid or from any screen that contains apps or widgets.

These actions are not just aesthetic though; personalizing the screens can make the things you use most often easily accessible and organized. For instance, you may want to move all your news, traffic, and weather apps to a secondary Home screen, while keeping Messaging, Books, Market, and Browser on the main one. You should also add widgets that you know you'll use often and remove ones you won't.

- -

WE ALREADY HAVE SOME THIRD-PARTY APPS; YOU MIGHT, TOO
The screen shots in this chapter include some third-party apps we've already acquired. You may have already acquired apps, too, or apps may have come preinstalled on your phone. All apps are listed together under the Open Apps icon, so what you see here and what you see on your own Droid will likely slightly differ.

- -

ADDING WIDGETS AND APPS

Although you haven't yet had a lot of experience with the apps available to you, especially the ones under the Open Apps icon (or the Applications icon on the Droid Charge), you may already have some idea of the apps you'll likely use the most. For instance, you may already know you want to have easy access to Email and Books, and you're already sure you won't want to tap the Open Apps icon every time you want to use them. You add apps to your Home screens from inside the All Apps window, as shown in Figure 2-1. After they're added, you can drag them to the wanted position.

FIGURE 2-1 Tap and hold any app in the All Apps window to add it to the Home screen.

To add an app to any screen, follow these steps:

1. Tap the Open Apps icon. (This icon is called Applications on the Droid Charge.)

2. Scroll through the apps until you find one you want to add.

3. Tap and hold the app.

4. On the Droid X2 and Droid 3, select Add to Home. You won't see this on the Droid Incredible 2 or the Droid Charge.

5. Drag the new icon to the wanted location and drop it there.

6. Repeat as wanted.

On the Droid X2 and the Droid 3, you probably noticed the Add to Group option in step 4. If you opt to create groups inside the All Apps window, you can add apps to that group to organize them. After you create a group, instead of All Apps as shown in Figure 2-1, you see the group name there instead. You can tap the arrow to see All Apps again or to access any other groups you create. You can start by placing apps you know you'll never use in a group named *Rarely Used*.

YOU MAY SEE MORE OPTIONS When you long tap an app in the All Apps window, you may see more options than Add to Home or Add to Group. You might see Share or Uninstall, for instance, if you've tapped a third-party app that supports these commands.

Beyond apps, you may also want to add specific widgets to your Home screens. You can add Android widgets no matter what phone you use, and you may have access to widgets provided by the phone manufacturer. Figure 2-2 shows two widget options on the Droid X2. You won't see the Motorola Widgets option on the Droid 3, Droid Incredible 2, or Droid Charge (or on another manufacturer's phone). Whatever the case, you can tap and hold an empty area of the screen to access this menu.

To add a widget to any screen, do this:

1. Tap and hold in an empty area of any screen.

2. Tap any of the widgets options. You may only have one, Widgets.

3. Tap the widget to add.

4. If there are options for the widget, such as where to search or what zip code to use, input the required information.

5. Repeat as wanted.

6. If you decide you don't want a widget on the screen, on most

FIGURE 2-2 Widgets are interactive versions of apps.

Droid models you can drag it to the top of the screen to the Trash icon. There's more on this later.

7. Remember, you can drag widgets from one area of the screen to another, or to another screen completely. Read on to learn more.

ADDING FOLDERS AND SHORTCUTS

You may have noticed in Figure 2-2 that you can add more than widgets. You can add Folders and Shortcuts, for instance. You can use a folder to group apps together, and shortcuts provide access to things you do often, such as make phone calls or look up contacts. To get to the screen shown in Figure 2-3 in the Droid X2, Droid 3, and Droid Charge, press the Menu button on your phone, tap Add, then tap Shortcuts. In the Droid Incredible 2, you tap the Personalize button instead of the Menu button.

To add a folder:

1. Press the Menu button, and tap Add. (On the Droid Incredible 2, tap the Personalize button.)

2. Tap Folder or Folders depending on the phone you have.

3. Tap New Folder (but note the other folders you can add).

4. Drag the folder to the wanted place on the screen.

5. Tap the folder to open it.

6. Tap and hold the folder's title bar for a second or two. (See Figure 2-4.)

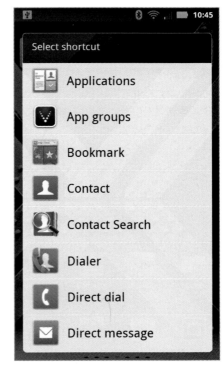

FIGURE 2-3 Create shortcuts to perform a task, such as make a phone call or send a direct message; use folders group apps.

Touch here

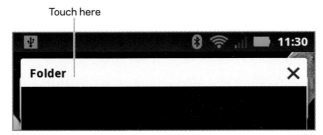

FIGURE 2-4 Tap the title bar of the open folder to access the options to rename them.

7. Type a new name for the folder.

8. Tap OK.

9. You can now reposition the folder and drag icons into it.

Try to drag your favorite apps into your new folder. Just touch and hold, and then drag and drop on the folder. You'll likely see some kind of animation; on the Droid X2 you see a folder opening. If you decide later you don't want the app there, simply repeat to drag it back!

To add a shortcut:

1. Tap and hold in an empty area of any screen.

2. Tap Shortcut or Shortcuts depending on the phone you have.

3. Select the shortcut to add.

4. If applicable, select additional options when prompted.

5. Repeat.

- -

CONSIDER ADDING THESE SHORTCUTS You can add a few shortcuts to your Home screen to simplify your life. When adding shortcuts, consider the following:

✦ On the Droid X2 and Droid 3, tap Dialer; then tap Recent Calls List. You have easy access to your most recent calls this way, and you won't need to open the Dialer to get to them.

✦ On the Droid X2, Droid 3, and Droid Charge, tap Applications; then tap your favorite application. On the Droid Incredible 2, access your favorite app by tapping App in the Personalization screen.

+ Tap Direct Dial, and select a contact you call often. Then you need tap only the icon on the Home screen to make the call.

+ On the Droid X2, Droid 3, and Droid Incredible 2, tap Music Playlist, and select your favorite. Again, you have easy access. Samsung decided not to include the Music Playlist on the Droid Charge and instead uses TuneWiki, a widget available in the Widgets list.

DELETING WIDGETS AND APPS

You might want to remove widgets and apps from your Droid screens for four reasons:

+ When adding apps and widgets in the previous section, you received a message stating a particular screen cannot accept any more apps or widgets because there is not enough room.

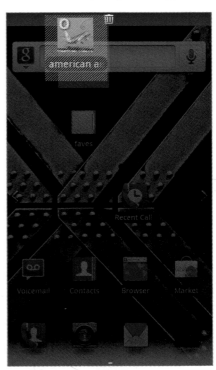

+ You added an app you now think you won't ever use.

+ You don't use a specific app and don't want it on the screen.

+ You added an app in the previous section, but realize the app is already available on the screen, and you have duplicates.

To remove an app (without uninstalling it), follow these steps:

1. Tap and hold the app to remove.

2. On the Droid X2 and Droid 3, drag it to the Trash icon that appears at the top of the screen. See Figure 2-5.

FIGURE 2-5 Tap, hold, and drag any app or shortcut to have access to the Trash.

3. On the Droid Incredible 2 and Droid Charge, drag it to the Remove icon at the bottom of the screen.

UNINSTALLING WIDGETS AND APPS

You can't uninstall the default widgets and apps, such as the Music app, Maps app, and Market app that shipped with your Droid. That's probably a security feature and a convenience for you and the programmers: If the Android programmers *had* allowed you to uninstall the default apps, they'd have to provide you a way to get them back if you change your mind or accidentally uninstall them! You can uninstall widgets and apps you've acquired yourself through the Market, though, and some of the third-party apps that came pre-installed on your phone. If you haven't yet obtained apps from the Market or you don't have any apps you want to uninstall, you can skip this section and come back to it when you need it. If you have installed apps and are ready to uninstall them, read on.

To uninstall an app and remove it completely from your Droid X2 or Droid 3 (which is different from simply removing it from a screen):

1. Tap the Open Apps icon.

2. Verify All Apps is selected. If it is not, tap the down arrow to select it.

3. Touch and hold the app to uninstall.

4. If Uninstall is an option, tap it. See Figure 2-6.

5. Tap OK to confirm.

6. Tap OK to return to the All Apps screen.

To access your list of applications on the Droid Incredible 2 or Droid Charge, follow these steps:

1. Press the Menu button.

2. Tap Settings.

3. Tap Applications.

4. Tap Manage Applications, as shown in Figure 2-7.

FIGURE 2-6 On the Droid X2 and Droid 3, you must uninstall apps from the Open Apps window.

5. Tap All from the button on top (with 4 squares on Incredible 2) to get a list of apps.

6. Select the individual app.

7. If the Uninstall option is available tap it.

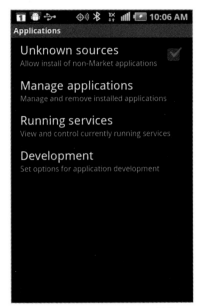

FIGURE 2-7 On the Droid Incredible 2 and Droid Charge, you must uninstall apps from the Manage Applications window.

REMOVE VERSUS UNINSTALL When you remove an app, you remove only its shortcut from the screen. The app remains available in the Open Apps window. When you uninstall an app, it is removed from the screen *and* from your Droid. You should uninstall apps you know you won't use to keep your Droid free of unwanted data and to keep your Droid's storage area from getting full.

REPOSITIONING APP SHORTCUTS AND WIDGETS

You might have positioned all the apps and widgets perfectly when you added them, but it's likely, after reviewing your work (and deleting items you didn't need), you now want to move some of them around. You can move an app or widget to a different area of a screen or to a different screen entirely, by tapping, holding, and then dragging it. Just drop it where you'd like it to appear.

Although the art of moving apps and widgets is a simple task, getting them perfectly organized might not be. Figure 2-8 shows how we've organized the Home screen on our Droid Incredible 2. Consider these tips when organizing your apps and widgets:

+ Place items you use regularly on the main Home screen.

+ Position widgets for Mail and Calendar, if you use them often, on the main Home screen.

+ Group news, weather, and traffic apps and widgets on a single, secondary screen.

+ Group entertainment apps and widgets together on a secondary screen.

+ Group reading apps together, including third-party apps you acquire such as Audible and Amazon Kindle.

+ Consider creating folders, as detailed earlier, to hold multiple, similar apps.

FIGURE 2-8 When you group apps together, they're easier to locate and manage.

REPLACING THE DEFAULT DOCK APPS

On the bottom of our two Motorola phones, the Droid X2 and the Droid 3, as well as the Samsung Droid Charge, the Dock is composed of four icons. You can replace these icons with the four apps you use most often. To replace any of these four icons on the Droid X2 or Droid 3:

1. Tap and hold the icon to change.

2. Tap the new icon to add to the Dock.

3. The new icon appears on the Dock and replaces the original. See Figure 2-9.

To replace any of the four icons on the Droid Charge:

1. Tap Applications.

2. Tap the Change Apps icon, which looks like a cog above the top-left app icon.

3. Tap and hold the icon to change.

4. Drag the icon on top of the icon in the Dock that you want to replace. The new icon appears on the Dock and replaces the original. See Figure 2-10.

FIGURE 2-9 The Dock can hold your favorite four apps; consider Dialer, Browser, Email, and Open Apps for now.

FIGURE 2-10 The Dock on the Droid Charge can hold your favorite four apps.

EXPLORE SCREEN OPTIONS IN SETTINGS While we're on the subject of changing how your screen looks, take a moment to review the options available in the Display area of the Settings app. To start, press the Menu button, tap Settings, and tap Display (or Display Settings on the Droid Charge). From there, consider changing the following:

+ **Brightness**—Enables your Droid to apply brightness settings automatically or for you to apply them manually.

+ **Auto-rotate screen**—Enables the Droid's screen to rotate automatically when you reposition it 90 or 180 degrees.

+ **Animation**—Enables all animations, some animations, or no animations. All Animations is the default. You could theoretically lengthen your Droid's battery life by disabling animations.

CHANGING THE WALLPAPER

The wallpaper is the picture or animation behind your apps and widgets. For now you can choose only a single wallpaper for your Droid, which is applied to every screen. Perhaps later you can configure a different image for each of the screens, but that's not currently the case.

Your Droid comes with *static* wallpapers (these are still pictures) and *live* wallpapers (wallpapers that actually move around behind your apps), and as you will see in Chapter 5 ("How Do I Get the Most from the Android Market?") you can obtain more. Additionally, you can use any picture in the Gallery as wallpaper. This means that you can take a picture with the Camera and use it as wallpaper, or you can use any picture you've copied to your Droid as wallpaper.

To explore and choose a new static wallpaper or a live one, follow these steps:

1. Press the Menu button.

2. On the Droid X2 and Droid 3, tap Add. On the Droid Charge and Droid Incredible 2, tap Wallpaper and go to step 4.

3. Tap Wallpapers.

4. Depending on the phone you have, tap Wallpapers, Wallpaper Gallery, or HTC Wallpapers.

5. Scroll through the options, and select one you like.

6. On the Droid X2, Droid 3, or Droid Charge, tap Set Wallpaper, as shown in Figure 2-11. On the Droid Incredible 2, all you need to do is tap the wallpaper you like.

7. Repeat steps 1, 2, and 3, and tap Live Wallpapers.

8. Scroll through and select a live wallpaper.

9. On the Droid X2 and Droid 3, tap Set Wallpaper. On the Droid Charge, tap the live wallpaper name or image in the list. On the Droid Incredible 2, tap the wallpaper you like.

FIGURE 2-11 Static wallpapers are simply pictures.

As you might guess, live wallpapers require your Droid's battery to work a little harder than it would if it were configured with a static one. However, for some, it's worth the trade-off.

- -

GET GREAT WALLPAPERS FROM THE MARKET If you didn't find anything that struck your fancy in the Wallpapers and Live Wallpapers sections on your Droid, you can likely find something you like in the Market. Refer to Chapter 5 to learn how to use the Market, and then search for wallpapers. For a bit of fun, make a note to look for Aquarium Live Wallpaper. There are some nice aquariums available!

- -

CHANGING THE RINGTONE

Another way to personalize your phone is to change the ringtone. This seems simple enough, but additional sound options are hidden with the ringtone settings. The best way to start on the Droid X2, Droid 3, or Droid Charge is to access the Settings app. You can do that from the All Apps or Applications icon or the Menu button. When in Settings, tap Sound or Sound Settings. When in the Sound Settings window, tap Phone Ringtone, select your favorite, and tap OK. The Droid Incredible 2 gives you a more direct method of changing the ringtone. All you have to do is tap the Personalize button, and then tap Ringtone. Tap your chosen ringtone in the list and then tap Apply, as shown in Figure 2-12.

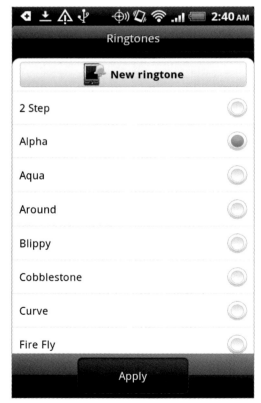

FIGURE 2-12 The list of ringtones available on the Droid Incredible 2.

EXPLORING OTHER SOUNDS

While in the Sound Settings window, scroll down to see other sound options. One is Audible Touch Tones. This is enabled on the Droid X2, Droid Incredible 2, and Droid Charge and plays tones when using the dial pad. Also by default, the phone vibrates only when the phone rings if Silent is the selected ring tone profile. You may want the phone to vibrate at every incoming call. There are additional sound settings to explore, including the sound that plays when a call is connected, among other things. Take the time now to explore the rest of the sound settings.

- -

EXPLORE PROFILES Press the Menu button on your Droid phone and tap Profiles, if it's available. You'll see profiles for Home, Work, and Weekend. You can switch among these profiles and customize them as you want to further personalize your phone.

- -

Getting Personal Data on Your Phone

You have data you want to put on your Droid, or data you want to access from it. You may have pictures, music, and video on a home computer you want to store on your Droid phone, for instance. Perhaps you have documents and spreadsheets you'd like to access while you're away from the office, which you store in online servers. You may have calendar data and contacts you'd like to incorporate as well. You probably want to have access to the pictures you store on Picasa or Facebook, too, as well as the information you have available on sites such as LinkedIn.

Unfortunately, there's no one-size-fits-all solution for making available every type of data you have for every scenario and phone. So before you start randomly copying, moving, or syncing data, (try to look at a few of the ways you can accomplish these tasks and decide what route you'd like to take. Additionally, find out how much space you have on your Droid for storing data; that's certainly important!

HOW MUCH DATA CAN MY DROID STORE?

Of the four phones used in this book, the Droid X2 and the Droid 3 have three places to store data: an area reserved for application storage, the internal storage area for your personal data, and storage you add by inserting an SD card. The Droid Incredible 2 and Droid Charge have two places: storage in an external SD card and internal phone storage.

Your phone, even if it isn't one of these, likely offers these areas, too. (You need to look at the documentation for your phone to be sure.) Following are what ours support:

+ **Droid X2**—Comes with up to 8GB of onboard storage and comes with an 8GB microSD card preinstalled. It supports up to a 32GB microSD card.

+ **Droid 3**—Comes with up to 16GB of onboard storage and supports up to a 32GB microSD card.

+ **HTC Droid Incredible 2**—Comes with up to 16GB of onboard storage and supports up to a 32GB microSD card.

+ **Samsung Droid Charge**—Comes with up to 2GB of onboard storage and includes a 32GB microSD card pre-installed.

To find out how much storage you have installed, and how much is still available on your Droid X2 and Droid 3, follow these steps:

1. Press the Menu button.

2. Tap Settings.

3. Tap Storage (you may have to scroll down). See Figure 2-13.

FIGURE 2-13 The Storage option shows how much space is available to you for storing personal data.

There you can find lots of information including the following:

+ **Application storage**—Your Droid's applications are stored here, and available space is offered.

+ **Internal storage**—Your Droid's total storage capacity is listed here along with the amount of available space. You can format this space if wanted.

+ **SD card**—The size of your Droid's SD card is offered here, along with how much available space is left.

On the Droid Incredible 2 and Droid Charge, to find out how much storage you have installed and how much is available, follow these steps:

1. Press the Menu button.

2. Tap Settings.

3. Tap SD & Phone Storage on the Droid Incredible 2 or SD Card & Phone Storage on the Droid Charge.

There you can find the following information, as shown in Figure 2-14:

+ **External SD card**—Your Droid's total storage capacity is listed here along with the amount of available space. You can also unmount the SD card for safe removal. After you unmount the card, you can format it if you want.

+ **Internal phone storage**—Your Droid's applications are stored here, and available space is shown.

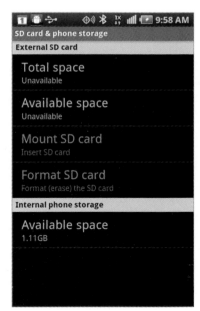

FIGURE 2-14 The SD card and phone storage screen shows how much space is available to you for storing personal data.

WHAT ARE MY DATA TRANSFER OPTIONS, IN A NUTSHELL?

As previously noted, you should consider and carefully weigh the options for getting data on your Droid before you haphazardly begin copying or syncing data to it. You should also be aware of how much data you want to transfer. Your Droid does have a limited amount of storage space; therefore , it may be best to save as much data as you can to online servers and access the data from there when you need it. Likewise, you can store data on your home computers and stream that data to your Droid using Digital Living Network Alliance (DLNA) technologies when you're within range.

The alternative to accessing data from another source when you need it is to copy the data to your Droid. For example, if your Droid has only 32GB of free space, and your Videos folder contains 200GB of movies, copying just won't work. Likewise, if you want to access data (such as documents and spreadsheets) from computers at your office and home, as well as on your Droid phone, it's probably best to store them in a single place to manage version control.

Following are your options to make data available on your Droid, in a nutshell:

+ **Using DLNA**—To use this feature, your phone must support DLNA and you must have at least one networked DLNA-compatible device on your wireless home network that contains shared media. Compatible devices include computers, game stations, media centers, televisions, and more. If you have compatible devices, you will select the desired device from a list of compatible devices on your phone (if there's more than one available), and then, you can easily copy data from those compatible devices to your phone. Better than that though, it's just as easy to stream data to your phone from the compatible devices or from your phone to them. Figure 2-15 shows the DLNA app on the Droid X2.

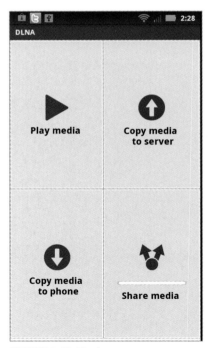

FIGURE 2-15 The best way to copy media to your phone, or to play shared media over a network, is to use DLNA.

✛ **Storing data using Google's part of the cloud**—This is another excellent option and should be combined with DNLA. You can sync, export/import, and upload data to your Google account from your home computer using various Google services, and that data will be available on your Droid the next time you connect to the Internet from it. For example, you can upload pictures to Google's Picasa, and those pictures will be available to you on your Droid from the Gallery app. You can upload documents from your computer to Google Documents, and they'll be available from Droid when you need them (as well as from other computers). You can export your address book from your home computer to your Gmail account and then access those contacts from your Droid phone. If you store data online, you must get online to access it!

✛ **Copying and pasting/dragging and dropping**—You can copy data stored on your computer to your Droid by connecting your Droid to it and then dragging and dropping or copying and pasting the data to the proper folders. This works well if you have a microSD card installed; otherwise, you may need a third-party file management app (depending on the model of your phone).

✛ **Syncing with a computer**—You can use Windows Media Sync to sync the media on your PC to your Droid phone. If you already use Media Player, certainly give it a shot.

Following are a few other options worth noting, but they aren't the best way to go and should be used as a last resort:

✛ **Emailing**—You can email data from your computer to your Gmail account. When it arrives, you can access and save certain attachments (not all). This works well only if you have a few items to move or copy and if you have the option to save the data you want to receive. If you need full attachment functionality, you need a file management app such as Astro and a productivity suite such as Documents To Go to make it work.

✛ **Downloading from the Internet**—If you have data stored on other Internet servers besides Google, you can download data from those servers to your Droid. For instance, you can tap any picture in your Facebook library, and tap Save Image to create a local copy. The quality is generally poor when you opt for this method.

USING DLNA

Because of the enormous amount of compatible devices that are DLNA-compatible, and because sharing your media over wireless networks using Macs and PCs also differs among operating systems and OS versions, we can't tell you how to set up and use DLNA from start to finish. However, we can tell you what you need to do and in what order. When your network is ready, your DLNA-compatible Droid will be ready, too.

Following is a list of things to do at home to make your media available to your Droid phone via the DLNA app:

1. Set up a wireless network at your home.

2. Purchase and install a DLNA-compatible device (costs will differ depending on what you decide to buy). Your PC or Mac may already be compatible, and PlayStation 3 and Xbox also work.

3. Put data on these devices, including music, video, pictures, and more.

4. Do what is necessary to share this data. Figure 2-16 shows how to start the sharing process using Windows Media Player.

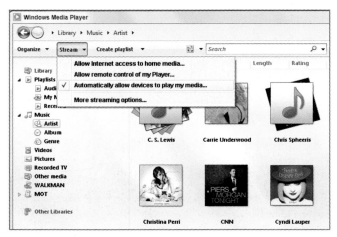

FIGURE 2-16 After you obtain media, share it with others.

5. Configure the device so it's capable of receiving media from your phone, if wanted. Sending media from your phone to a network share is an option on your Droid.

6. Leave the device turned on, and make sure it's awake and ready.

When your network is ready, you're ready. From your DLNA-compliant Droid phone, follow these steps:

1. Tap the Open Apps button.

2. Tap DLNA.

3. If prompted to approve access to your device from a device on your network, tap Accept or Decline.

4. Decide what you want to do, and tap the option (these options can vary, depending on the phone):

   A. **Play media**—Play media currently stored on any of your compliant network devices on your phone. This does not copy the media to your phone.

   B. **Copy media to server**—Copy media on your phone to a compliant device on your network. This does not remove the media from your phone.

   C. **Copy media to phone**—Copy media from a compliant network device to your phone.

   D. **Share media**—Allow others with compliant devices to access the media on your phone.

5. When prompted to choose a device to connect to, make the appropriate choice by tapping.

6. Drill into the folder that contains the media to play, and tap it. See Figure 2-17.

FIGURE 2-17 This music is on a network computer but can be played on the Droid via streaming and DLNA.

USING THE CLOUD

Although uploading or syncing data from your computer to Google Services such as Google Calendar, Contacts, Picasa, and the like might take some time, it's ultimately the best way to go with Droid. After you import this data, you can access it from your Droid, from your computer, from your smartphone, or anywhere else you can access the Internet. But it isn't just that. If you ever lose your Droid and buy another (or upgrade to a newer device), all you have to do to make the data you uploaded available on your new device is to sign in with your Google account.

Although it would be impossible to detail every option for importing personal data to your Google account using the cloud, we'll walk you through using Picasa, and you can hopefully draw on that to upload additional information. With that done, you will learn how to add accounts to your Droid for your other online entities, so you'll have access to personal data, too, including LinkedIn, Facebook, and Twitter.

CLOUD SERVERS Google gives you some storage space to use for free, specifically 1024MB, or in layman's terms, about a gigabyte. If you need more you can buy more here: `www.google.com/accounts/PurchaseStorage`. At the present time you can add (per year) the following:

+ 20GB for $5
+ 80GB for $20
+ 200GB for $50
+ 400GB for $100
+ 1TB (that's 1,000 GB) for $256

Upload Pictures with Picasa

Picasa is one way to get photos from your desktop computer to your Droid. It's a cloud service provided by Google. Although lots of other third-party options exist, Picasa, your Google account, and the Droid play well together. (This means they're compatible.) Thus, you'll have fewer headaches in the long run if you simply set up Picasa on your computer now, figure out what photos you'd like on your Droid, and send that data to the cloud for syncing.

To start using Picasa to upload photos, follow these steps:

1. From your home computer (or whatever computer holds the majority of your photos), visit http://picasa.google.com.

2. Download and install the latest Picasa software.

3. During the installation process, tell Picasa that you want it to locate all the photos on your computer and categorize them however it deems fit. Depending on how many photos you have, it could take Picasa quite a bit of time to complete this task.

4. When that's done, click a folder to sync.

5. Click Share, and Enable Sync. See Figure 2-18.

6. Log in with your Google username and password.

7. Click Sync.

Make sure, when you're deciding what to sync, that you select folders one at a time, and then click Share, and Enable Sync. This places the photos you'd like to store on Google's servers, and therefore, are the photos that will be synced to your Droid.

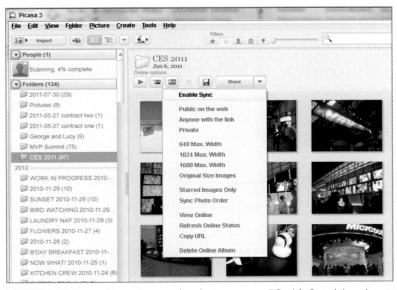

FIGURE 2-18 Set up Picasa to sync the photos on your PC with Google's web servers, and you'll have access to them on your Droid.

LOCATE YOUR PICASA PHOTOS ON YOUR DROID To view the photos you've synced through Picasa to Google's web servers using your Droid, follow these steps:

1. Tap Gallery.
2. Tap Online.
3. Browse the new folders that appear.

Adding Accounts for LinkedIn, Facebook, and Twitter

You can access other online data from your Droid. One way is to configure the accounts you own besides Google, namely LinkedIn, Facebook, and Twitter. Like many other techniques, these don't store data on your Droid but rather simply offer access to the data you store in the cloud.

To add an account to your Droid, follow these steps:

1. Press the Menu button.
2. Tap Settings.
3. Tap Accounts or Accounts & Sync, depending on the phone you have.
4. Tap Add Account.
5. Tap an option. See Figure 2-19. On some phones, green check boxes appear next to the accounts already installed on your phone.
6. Type your email address and password, tapping Next and Done as applicable.
7. Tap Done.
8. Repeat as necessary to add additional accounts.

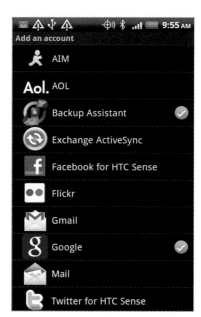

FIGURE 2-19 When you add accounts here, you have access to them on your Droid.

9. Press the Home button when finished.

10. To see your new messages, pull down on the Status bar. Tap any option. You can see your new alerts and notifications for the app.

Now, tap the Open Apps icon, and tap Social Networking. Tap All Services, and choose what services you'd like to view, as shown in Figure 2-20. For now, this may suffice and meet your social networking needs. Later, refer to Chapter 5 to see how you can obtain apps for these newly added accounts that can provide more functionality. You can then refer to Chapter 8 ("How Do I Get the Most from Social Media Integration?") to learn more.

FIGURE 2-20 Apps from the Market can enhance how you use social networking information.

COPYING AND PASTING

To copy and paste (or drag and drop) data from a computer to a Droid phone, you must first physically connect it using the supplied USB cable. You also need to tell your Droid you want its storage card to act as a mass storage device your computer can access. Finally, you must make sure the Droid drivers install properly on the computer. Figure 2-21 shows what you want to see when connecting your Droid. After you copy the data, you can view and access it from the Files app.

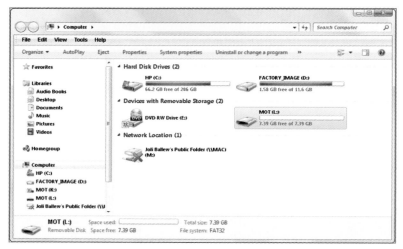

FIGURE 2-21 If configured properly, you can drill into your Droid's storage areas to drag and drop data.

On the Motorola Droid X2 or Droid 3, follow these steps:

1. Connect your Droid to your computer using the supplied USB cable.

2. Pull down on the phone's Status bar, and tap USB Connection.

3. Choose USB Mass Storage, and tap OK. See Figure 2-22.

4. Open an explorer window on your computer.

FIGURE 2-22 To enable dragging and dropping, choose USB mass storage.

5. Browse to the location of the phone (refer to Figure 2-21).

6. Open your phone's storage folder by double-clicking it.

7. Drag wanted data there, preferably by dragging folders of related data. See Figure 2-23.

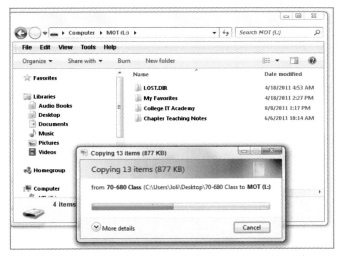

FIGURE 2-23 Drag data to the new folders (or copy and paste).

On the Motorola Droid Incredible 2 and Droid Charge, follow these steps:

1. Connect your Droid to your computer using the supplied USB cable. If you use a Droid Charge, skip ahead to step 4.

2. Tap the Status bar, leave your finger on it, and then pull down on the phone's Status bar.

3. Tap Connect to PC. See Figure 2-24.

4. An explorer window opens on your computer, and a drive that contains your phone's storage folder appears as shown earlier in Figure 2-21.

FIGURE 2-24 Enable dragging and dropping by tapping Connect to PC.

5. Drag the desired data there, preferably by dragging folders of related data as shown earlier in Figure 2-23.

To access the data from your Droid, follow these steps:

1. Disconnect your phone from the computer.
2. Tap the Open Apps icon.
3. Tap Files.
4. Note the new files, and tap each to see if and how it opens.

- -

UNDERSTANDING COMPATIBILITY You can use your Droid phone to open lots of types of data, from picture files to documents to spreadsheets. It can play most music files and many types of video. Because we don't have room here to list every compatible file type, you can discover what works and what doesn't. If you decide a file won't play, delete it from the device, and note the incompatible file type. Just because a file won't play the first time you try doesn't mean it will never play, though. For instance, a file might not play because you don't have the appropriate app. As an example, to play Audible audio books, you need the Audible app, and you need to sign in with it.

- -

SYNCING WITH MEDIA PLAYER

If you use Windows Media Player and you have a compatible Droid phone, you can sync your Droid with your computer using the Sync option in the Media Player program. This is often better than dragging and dropping, because media is placed where it should be placed, and can be found by your Droid easily. If DLNA is not an option, or if you like Windows Media Player, this might be the option for you.

To set up your Droid for syncing with Windows Media Player, follow these steps:

On the Motorola Droid X2 or Droid 3:

1. Connect your Droid to your computer using the supplied USB cable.
2. Pull down on the phone's Status bar, and tap USB connection.
3. Tap Windows Media Sync, and tap OK.

At your computer:

1. Open Windows Media Player.
2. Click the Sync tab.
3. Drag the media to sync with your Droid. See Figure 2-25.
4. Click Start Sync.

FIGURE 2-25 Choose what to sync with Windows Media Player.

On the Droid Incredible 2:

1. Connect your Droid to your computer using the supplied USB cable.
2. Pull down on the phone's Status bar, and then tap USB connection.
3. Tap Media Sync and then tap Done.

At your computer:

1. Click Sync digital media files to this device using Windows Media Player in the AutoPlay window.
2. Click the Sync tab.
3. Drag the media to sync with your Droid. See Figure 2-26.
4. Click Start Sync.

FIGURE 2-26 Drag the media files to sync with your Droid into the Sync list.

- -

WINDOWS MEDIA PLAYER DOESN'T RECOGNIZE MY DROID CHARGE. WHAT DO I DO? The Droid Charge doesn't natively sync to media players as do the other Droid models covered in this book. You can download a Windows Media Player synchronization app from the Android Market that will fill the gap. Open the Market by tapping Market on the Home screen. Tap the Search icon in the upper right corner of the screen and then tap Windows media player. After you tap Windows media player in the list, you'll see available sync apps at the top of the screen you can consider.

- -

If the data you sync is compatible, you can find it on your Droid in its related app. For instance, in Figure 2-27 the Music app is open, and you can see the artists we've synced. You can't see the audiobooks, though. For that, we'll need to acquire or open a compatible app. In this case, that's the Audible app. Refer to the "Understanding Compatibility" note for a bit more insight.

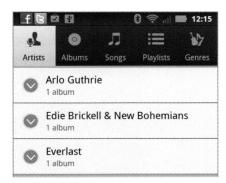

FIGURE 2-27 The Music app with synced artists in the list.

Related Questions

❖ Where is my music and how do I play it? **PAGE 247**

❖ Where are my photos and how do I view them? **PAGE 230**

❖ Where are my videos and how do I watch them? **PAGE 266**

CHAPTER THREE

HOW DO I USE THE PHONE AND MANAGE CONTACTS?

Y ou might find it odd that you're three chapters into this book and haven't learned how to make a phone call or manage contacts. That's because you use your smartphone for so much more! You often want to get online and surf the web, first and foremost, and you want to customize your phone and put your own data on it next. Making phone calls is often an afterthought: a simple feature you expect to be available and only use when you have to.

Making and Answering Phone Calls

Android phones support several technologies for making phone calls. You can also use these technologies to connect to the Internet when Wi-Fi isn't available or if Wi-Fi is disabled, although it counts as data usage against your data plan. The Status bar that runs across the top of your Droid shows how you are currently connected to a network; you learned a little about these icons in Chapter 2 ("How Do I Make the Droid Uniquely Mine?").

REVIEWING ROAMING SETTINGS

With most cellular data plans, you get charged extra to roam. If you do see Roaming (or Roam) on the Status bar, be mindful. It means you're not connected to Wi-Fi, and you're outside your provider's coverage area.

Before you regularly start using your phone, consider setting roaming safeguards. To do this on four of the most popular Droid phones, follow these steps:

1. Press the Menu button and tap Settings.

2. Tap Wireless & Network Settings (or whatever option is appropriate for your phone).

3. Tap Mobile Networks. See Figure 3-1.

FIGURE 3-1 All the Droid phones offer the Mobile Networks options.

4. On the Droid X2:

   A. Tap System Select. Tap Home Only to disable roaming.

5. On the Droid 3:

   A. Tap Mobile Networks. Roaming options might be grayed out on your phone. If enabled on yours, configure as wanted.

6. On the Droid Incredible 2:

   A. Tap CDMA Options.

   B. Tap System Select. Tap Home Only to disable roaming.

7. On the Droid Charge:

   A. Tap System Selection.

   B. Tap CDMA Mode.

   C. Tap Home Only to disable roaming.

WHAT HAPPENS IF I'M IN A CALL AND I LEAVE THE CELLULAR NETWORK COVERAGE AREA? With many providers, if you leave a coverage area while in a call (and roaming is disabled), the call drops. You can try several things if this happens. You can enable roaming and place a new call, return to a coverage area, or turn your phone off and back on. The latter technique doesn't often work, but you may just pick up a new signal that isn't roaming!

USING THE PHONE

All the Droid phones have a Dialer or Phone icon on the Home screen. Figure 3-2 shows the Phone app on the Droid Incredible 2. All Droid models covered in this book have the Dialer icon on the Dock.

To make a phone call, you need to tap the Dialer or Phone icon, verify the Dialer tab or Keypad icon is selected, and type the phone number using the keypad. (There is no tab or icon on the Droid Incredible 2.) Generally after that, you tap the Green Phone icon or Call, as shown in Figure 3-2. (It turns red and you can press that to end a call.)

FIGURE 3-2 The Phone app on the Droid Incredible 2 enables you place calls by dialing them manually, choosing from the recent call list, or accessing contacts you've input or acquired.

No one wants to type in a phone number manually though, especially if it's a person you call a lot.

USING YOUR VOICE TO MAKE CALLS When in the Dialer app, look for a microphone. (Sorry, Droid Incredible 2 users, but this feature isn't available on your phone.) Tap it once and then speak a command. Try "Call" and then say a number out loud. You must answer Yes or No if prompted by the phone to verify your command. You can also use this option to call a contact by name, redial, or perform other tasks.

VIEWING YOUR CALL HISTORY

If you've already placed a few calls, you can view your call history and tap any item in it to place a call to that number again. On the Droid X2 and Droid 3, that tab is called Recent. As you can see in Figure 3-3, the first call we made on our new phone was to 555-555-5555, and this number was not known to the phone. We had not created a contact for it. We used a similar fake number to be the number for a cat named Pico Ballew, and now, when a call is placed, the contact picture we created for the contact is shown, and the phone understands who that number belongs to.

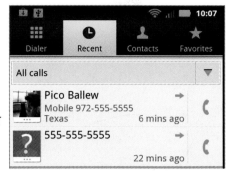

FIGURE 3-3 The Recent tab enables you to easily access previously dialed numbers.

On the Droid Incredible 2, tap the Call history icon at the bottom right of the screen (it's to the right of the Call button). On the Droid Charge, tap Call Log at the top of the screen to view your call history.

HOLDING A CONFERENCE CALL

When in a call you can add another person, if your Droid and data plan support this. Figure 3-4 shows the option to add another call to an existing one, and Figure 3-5 shows the option to merge those calls when connected. These screenshots use a Droid 3.

To add a second person to a phone call:

1. Tap Dialer on the Home screen.

2. Place a phone call using any method.

3. When connected, tap Add Call, as shown in Figure 3-4. Continue to Step 5.

FIGURE 3-4 While in a call, if Add (or Add Call) is an option, you can tap it to add another person to the call.

4. For the Droid Incredible 2 and Droid Charge:

   A. On the Droid Incredible 2, tap Settings and then tap Add Call.

   B. On the Droid Charge, tap Add Call.

5. When prompted, tap Merge, as shown in Figure 3-5.

FIGURE 3-5 When you merge two phone calls, you create a conference call.

REVIEW YOUR DATA PLAN It's smart to occasionally review your data plan and check to see if a different plan is available that may suit your needs more effectively. You can easily do this by calling your provider, often for free by dialing 611 from your phone. It's also a good idea to check your usage a few times a month the first few months of your service agreement to make sure you do not exceed any limits.

ANSWERING, SWAPPING, HOLDING, MUTING, AND MORE

As you talk more and more on your phone, you encounter more and more icons you can tap. For instance, if your phone is inactive when a call comes in, you likely need to move a slider on the lock screen to get to it. After you activate the phone, you can opt to receive it. Figure 3-6 shows this option.

FIGURE 3-6 When a call comes in, you can answer it or ignore it.

You encounter these commands and possibly others as the Droid evolves:

+ **Ignore**—If you opt to ignore a call, it will be sent to voicemail.

+ **Swap Calls (or Swap)**—If you're already in a call and another comes in, you see an option to swap to the new call if you have the feature enabled through your data plan. When you swap a call, the person on the first call is placed on hold. You can swap back when wanted.

+ **Mute**—When in a call, Mute becomes available (refer to Figure 3-5). It's easy to tap Mute while in a call, and thus keep the other party from hearing what you say.

+ **Dialpad**—Another item you see while in a call is the option to access the Dialpad. This is important because you often are prompted to Press 1 to Continue or Press 0 for Operator.

Finally, you can also use the phone while in a call. Just press the Home button on the phone to access the Home screen. If time allows, make a few phone calls now, and have a few people call you. It won't take long to get a feel for how the phone features of your Droid work.

- -

USING SETTINGS IN THE DIALER APP When in the Dialer app, you can press the Menu button to access additional settings. What you see depends on the screen you're on, and possibly your Droid model. Explore what is offered on your phone when time allows.

- -

Creating and Using Contacts

The Contacts app is a separate app, available from the All Apps menu, which you can add to your Home screen using the techniques you learned in Chapter 2. However, you don't need to use this app. You can use the Dialer! Just tap the Dialer icon that's already on the Dock, and tap the Contacts tab. You may find, as shown in Figure 3-7, that you already have some contacts listed. The reason this happens, for the most part, is that you had contacts already associated with your Google or Gmail account, and when you logged in with those credentials, the contacts were automatically synced to your phone.

On the Droid X2, Droid 3, and Droid Charge, the functionality is very similar. Just under the Contacts tab you can see the options you need to create and access contact groups, search for contacts, and add new contacts. If wanted, tap these now (and then tap the Back button on the phone) to return to this screen. Tap the icon that looks like two heads to access Groups; tap the magnifying glass to search for contacts; and tap the + sign to add a contact.

The functionality on the Droid Incredible 2 is different from the other Droids discussed in this book. When you're in the Dialer, press Menu and then tap People. You can add a contact on the All screen, tap the Contacts icon at the bottom of the screen (which looks like one Rolodex card in front of another) to view groups, and you can press Search to search for names in your Contacts list.

You learn how to perform the tasks associated with these icons on your specific phone later in this chapter.

CREATING A CONTACT

You may already have contacts on your phone. However, you still need to know how to manually add contacts. If you have more than one account in use on your phone, you'll be prompted to associate the new contact with one of them first.

FIGURE 3-7 The Contacts tab offers various ways to group, access, and manage contacts.

TURN OFF TEXT OR WORD PREDICTION BEFORE TYPING NAMES By default your Droid enables text or word prediction for your keyboard. (The term depends on the Droid you're using.) That is, when you type a word the Droid will automatically try to figure out what word you're trying to type. This is an effort to make things easier for you when you're typing on the Droid's small screen. When you're typing names, though, having word prediction enabled can result in word replacements that can be humorous and aggravating. (For example, the Droid replaced "Butow" with "Button" when I entered a contact for a relative.) You can turn off word or text prediction in the Language & Settings or Language & Keyboard section on the Settings screen. In this section on the Droid Incredible 2 tap Touch Input, tap Text Input, and then tap Prediction; on the Droid Charge tap Swype and then tap Word Prediction. On the Droid X2 and the Droid 3, explore these: Input Method, Swype, Multi-touch Keyboard, and Built-in Keyboard, as applicable.

To manually add a contact on the Droid X2 or Droid 3:

1. Open Contacts or the Dialer app.

2. Tap the Contacts tab if applicable.

3. Tap the + sign. Then:

   ✚ If your Google account is the only account you've configured on your Droid, a new, blank, Contact Card opens.

   ✚ If you've added additional accounts, such as a corporate account or secondary personal account, set up some kind of backup assistant, or have another compatible third-party app installed, you'll be prompted as to which account to associate the new contact with. Choose it and tap OK.

4. In the New Contact window, type the wanted information, tapping Next when necessary. Add as much as you can, including the contact's full name, email address, physical address, phone number, and any other information.

5. If wanted, tap the photo placeholder, as shown in Figure 3-8, and either take a picture or locate one to apply. The steps may differ from phone to phone, but you'll be guided through this if you opt to do it now.

6. When finished, tap Done and then Save.

You can also add a contact to your Contact list using the information in an email you receive. This isn't detailed here because the

FIGURE 3-8 When adding a contact, add as much information as possible.

email app options and how to use them hasn't been discussed, but you can use it to add contact information to your Droid.

To add a contact manually on your Droid Charge or Incredible 2, follow these steps:

1. Tap the Phone app on the Dock.

2. Open your Contacts list as follows:

    A. On the Droid Incredible 2, press Menu and then tap People.

    B. On the Droid Charge, tap Contacts.

3. Tap Add Contact or the + sign depending on the Droid you use. Then:

    + If your phone account is the only account you've configured on your Droid, a new, blank, Contact Card opens.

    + If you've added additional accounts, such as a Google account or secondary personal account, set up some kind of backup assistant, or have another compatible third-party app installed, you'll be prompted as to which account to associate the new contact with. Tap the account to use.

4. In the New Contact window, type the wanted information. Add as much as you can, including the contact's full name, email address, physical address, phone number, and any other information.

5. If wanted, tap the photo placeholder, as shown in Figure 3-9, and either take a picture or locate one to apply. The steps may differ from phone to phone, but you'll be guided through this if you opt to do it now.

6. When finished, tap Save.

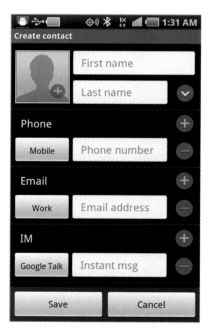

FIGURE 3-9 The photo placeholder on the Droid Charge New Contact window enables you to add a photo to the contact card.

LOCATE A CONTACT AND ACCESS OPTIONS To locate a contact, open the appropriate app (Contacts or Dialer). Then scroll through the contact list, tap a letter on the right side to jump to that letter in the list, or tap the Search icon. You can also press the Search button on your phone. After you select a contact, you can access options such as View contact, Call contact, Text contact, Add to Favorites, Edit Contact, and Delete Contact by tapping and holding a contact name.

SYNCING YOUR CONTACTS TO GOOGLE

You have contacts in many places. You may have contacts associated with a third-party email account that's not web-based (such as Time Warner), with your contacts stored only on your computer (perhaps in Microsoft Outlook). You could have contacts on other tablets, other phones, laptops, or desktop PCs or Macs. You may have an online address book at AOL or through another third-party web-based email client such as Yahoo!. Getting those contacts on your Droid can be a trying experience.

You can use Google's cloud services to get many of those contacts on your Droid. You know that the contacts you associate with your Google account will be automatically synced to your Droid, no matter how they get there. This opens up a solution for those hard-to-sync accounts. You can upload or sync contacts in other places to Google, and then, those contacts will appear on your Droid under your Google account.

The directions for transferring this data vary by provider, device, and email client, so you need to review the tools available at `http://mail.google.com/support/`. Do this from a desktop or laptop computer. Choose Import Email and Contacts. When there, locate the Help file that best suits your needs.

HOW DO I TRANSFER CONTACTS ON AN EXISTING SIM CARD TO MY DROID? To get contact data from a SIM card you use on a different device to your Droid, you have to somehow export those contacts from the SIM card (device) to a computer and then import them to Google. When associated with your Gmail account, they will be synced to your Droid. If you try to do this yourself, you'll likely need to acquire and install some kind of syncing software for your computer.

Before you try the do-it-yourself approach though, we've had great luck by physically visiting the provider's store (in our case, Verizon) and asking them for help. They often have the software and hardware required to perform this task and will do it for free.

EDITING AND DELETING CONTACTS

Information about your contacts can change, and you need to quickly replace older information with newer information. You should input as much infor-

mation as possible when creating and editing contacts because you can use that information to easily communicate with them or find them, often by simply tapping a piece of data you've added. For instance, if you've added an email address, you can tap it, and your email app opens with the contact name already in the To line. If you've added a website address, you can also tap that, and the Browser opens to the web page!

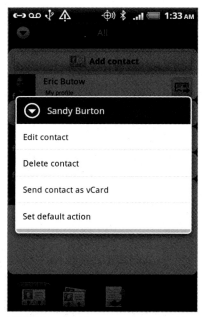

To edit a contact, follow these steps on all Droid models:

1. Open the Contacts or People app.

2. Use any technique to locate the contact.

3. Tap and hold the contact name.

4. Tap Edit or Edit Contact. See Figure 3-10.

FIGURE 3-10 When you tap and hold a contact name, options appear.

5. Use the keypad or keyboard to move through the contact information, adding it as needed. Tap the Plus sign by any entry to add more information. See Figure 3-11.

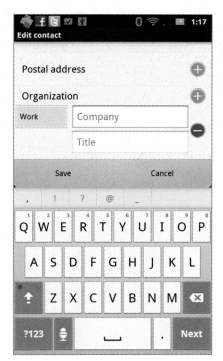

FIGURE 3-11 Plus signs enable you to add more information.

ADDING A CONTACT AS A FAVORITE

Now take a break from all this complicated syncing and editing for a moment, and perform a simple task: Make a contact a favorite. When a contact is a favorite, you can access it quickly from the Favorites tab in the Contacts or Dialer app.

I DON'T SEE MY CONTACT IN THE LIST. HOW DO I MAKE THAT PERSON A FAVORITE? You can only designate a saved Contact in your list as a favorite. If you don't see your contact name, that means you need to enter it first and save it. Then you can follow the steps below to add that contact as a favorite.

To make a contact a favorite on the Droid X2, Droid 3, and Droid Charge, follow these steps:

1. Locate the contact to add.
2. Tap and hold.
3. Tap Add to Favorites. See Figure 3-12.

If you have a Droid Incredible 2, here's how to make a favorite:

1. Locate the contact to add.
2. Tap and hold.
3. Tap Edit Contact.
4. Scroll down until you see Group, as shown in Figure 3-13.
5. Tap None, and then tap Favorites in the Pick Group(s) menu.

Now, consider adding a shortcut for Favorites to the Home screen:

+ On the Droid X2 or Droid 3, press the Menu button, tap Settings, and tap Shortcuts. Choose Dialer and then Favorites.

+ On the Droid Incredible 2, tap Personalize, tap Folder, and then tap Starred.

+ On the Droid Charge, tap and hold on an empty area on the Home screen. Tap Folders and then tap Starred Contacts.

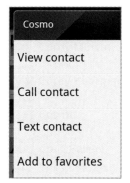

FIGURE 3-12 Add contacts to the Favorites tab to have quick access.

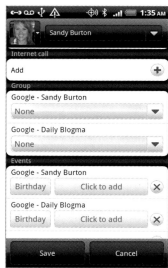

FIGURE 3-13 Pick the Favorites for the contact by tapping None and then tapping Favorites.

CALLING OR EMAILING A CONTACT

You learn in various places in this book how to communicate with contacts. In the Gmail app, when composing an email message, you have to start typing only a contact's name, and choices appear from your Contacts list. In Google

Talk, you can easily invite people to chat by typing in their names (which again, are available from Contacts). You'll see a lot of this as you get to know your Droid phone. You know you don't just communicate with contacts from outside the Contacts app, though; there are many ways to communicate with contacts from within it. As you've learned, you can use the list of contacts you have to make a phone call, send an email, and more.

When you access any Contact card in the Contacts app, almost all the information available responds to your tap:

✚ Tap the Green Phone icon to place a call. See Figure 3-14.

✚ Tap the Mail icon to send a quick text. Refer to Figure 3-14.

✚ Tap a physical address to open Maps and get directions to it.

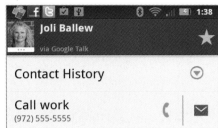

FIGURE 3-14 The Contact card offers many ways to quickly communicate with a contact.

✚ Tap a URL to open the Browser and visit the contact's website.

✚ Tap the email address to open an email program and start a new email message.

✚ Tap the round green circle to chat with Google Talk. If you see a Video Camera icon, you can video chat. Video chatting is not yet widely supported but should be in the near future. See Figure 3-15.

✚ Tap additional data as you acquire third-party apps that can be used with it (such as Jabber for texting).

FIGURE 3-15 If you see a green circle, you can contact that person via text.

APPLYING PERSONALIZED RINGTONES FOR A CONTACT

You may want to know who is calling without having to pick up your phone and look at the screen. The only way to do that is to configure a contact with a personalized ringtone. After it's configured, when that contact calls your phone, the personalized ringtone plays. Unfortunately, on the Droid X2 and Droid 3, it's not intuitive.

To apply a personalized ringtone for the Droid X2 and the Droid 3, follow these steps:

1. Open the Dialer app, and tap the Contacts tab.

2. Tap the contact once, with a quick tap.

3. Press the Menu button and tap Options, as shown in Figure 3-16.

4. On the next screen, tap Ringtone.

5. Choose a ringtone from the list, and tap OK. See Figure 3-17.

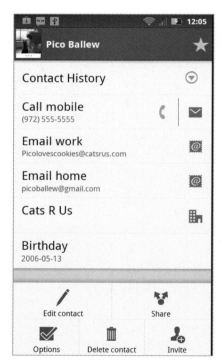

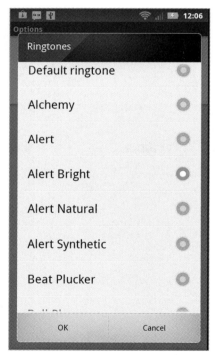

FIGURE 3-16 The option to set a personalized ringtone is under Options on the Droid X2 and Droid 3.

FIGURE 3-17 Your Droid phone comes with various ringtones to choose from, and you can get more from the Market.

Following is how to do this on the Incredible 2 and Charge:

1. Tap the Contacts or People icon.

2. Tap the contact once with a quick tap. If you use the Droid Incredible 2, skip to Step 4.

3. Press Menu and then tap Edit.

4. Scroll down the contact information page until you see the Ringtone option, as shown in Figure 3-18.

5. Tap Ringtone and then Phone Ringtone if necessary.

6. Tap different ringtones in the list. You can listen to each one you tap so that you can determine if the ringtone is right for you.

7. Tap OK.

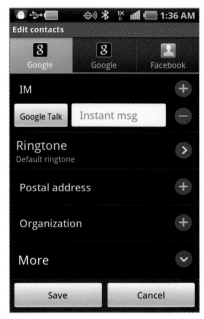

FIGURE 3-18 The Ringtone option enables you to select a personalized ringtone for each contact that calls you.

GETTING CREATIVE WITH RINGTONES If you have an aging parent, teenager, or other important contact, you may want to make sure that you can audibly distinguish when that person calls. We have set the traditional telephone ring set to play when our parents call, for instance. However, you can do more if you have the time. Set your vet's ringtone to the song "Who Let the Dogs Out?", or your exercise trainer's ringtone to "Burn, Baby, Burn."

Managing Contacts

If you have only a few contacts, managing them is no problem. If you have hundreds of contacts, you'll probably start looking for some way to group them. For instance, if you are the coach for a sports team and want to send a group email, unless you've grouped the contacts together, you must enter each name separately every time. If you create a group, you can send an email or a message to that group with a single tap. You can also easily add members to the group, create a group event with the Calendar app, and more. See Figure 3-19.

You can manage contacts in additional ways. If you have duplicate contacts you want to link together as one, you can "join" the contact with another. You can delete duplicate contacts or those you don't communicate with anymore. You can share contacts with others. There's quite a bit more than that though, as you'll become aware when you work through this section.

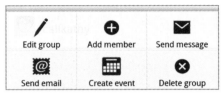

FIGURE 3-19 When you create a group of contacts, you can work with them as a whole.

GROUPING CONTACTS

Grouping contacts is one way to manage your contacts so they are easier to access and communicate with. Think for a moment about how your contacts are related, and consider the groups you could create. *Family* might be a good group to create, as is the name of any team you participate in, any group of employees at work, or any professional club or organization you manage or belong to.

To create a new group on your Droid X2 or Droid 3, follow these steps:

1. Open the Dialer or the Contacts app.

2. Tap the Contacts tab if necessary.

3. Tap the Groups icon; on these two phones it looks like two heads. See Figure 3-20.

4. Tap the + sign to add a new group.

5. Type a name for the group and tap OK. See Figure 3-21.

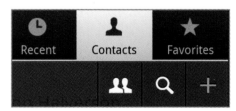

FIGURE 3-20 Here you can see the Groups icon, the Search icon, and the icon for adding a contact.

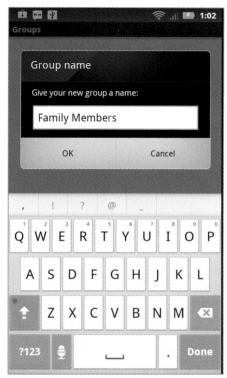

FIGURE 3-21 Name your group so that it's easily recognizable.

6. Tap each contact to add.

7. Tap Done when finished. See Figure 3-22.

8. With the group still on the screen, press the Menu button. Note what you can do:

   A. Edit a group.

   B. Add a member.

   C. Send a message.

   D. Send an email.

   E. Create an event.

   F. Delete a group.

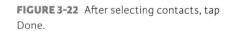

FIGURE 3-22 After selecting contacts, tap Done.

9. Press the Back button three times to return to the main Contacts screen.

To create a group and add members using the Droid Charge:

1. Open the Phone or the Contacts app.

2. Tap the Contacts tab if necessary.

3. Tap the Groups icon, which looks like two heads. See Figure 3-23.

4. Press Menu and then tap Create.

5. Type a name for the group.

6. Select the ringtone so that you hear the same ringtone from any contact in the group. See Figure 3-24.

7. Tap Save.

8. Tap the group name in the Contacts list.

FIGURE 3-23 The Groups icon appears in the icon bar that also includes Contacts, History, and Activities.

FIGURE 3-24 Name your group and select a unique ringtone so that the group and calls from members within it are easily recognizable.

9. Tap Add Member to view a list of members who can join your group.

10. Tap the member or members to add to your group. See Figure 3-25. If you want all available members to join, tap Select All. If you don't see your contact in the list, type in the Search Contacts box.

11. Tap Add.

12. With the group still on the screen, press the Menu button. Note what you can do:

    A. Edit a group.

    B. Add a member.

    C. Remove a member.

    D. Send a message.

    E. Send an email.

13. Press the Back button twice to return to the Groups screen. Return to the Contacts screen by tapping Contacts.

To create a group and add members using the Droid Incredible 2, follow these steps:

1. Open the Phone or the People app.

2. Press the Menu button, and then tap People if necessary.

3. Tap the Groups icon, which looks like one Contact card behind another. See Figure 3-26.

4. Tap Add Group.

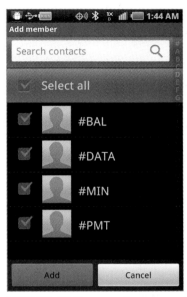

FIGURE 3-25 You can select one, multiple, or all users to join your group.

FIGURE 3-26 The Groups icon appears in the icon bar that also contains All Contacts and Call History.

5. Tap the name of the group on the Add Group screen, as shown in Figure 3-27.

6. Tap Add Contact to Group.

7. Scroll to the contact you want to add, and then tap the contact name.

8. Tap Save. The contact name appears in the Groups list.

9. Tap Save. The group appears in your Groups list. See Figure 3-28.

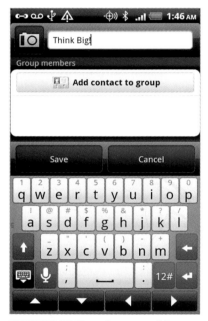

FIGURE 3-27 Type the name of the new group in the box at the top of the Add Group screen.

FIGURE 3-28 The new group appears in the Groups list and shows the number of contacts in the list in parentheses after the group name.

SORTING CONTACTS USING GROUPS

The whole point to creating groups and placing contacts into them is so that you can easily sort your contacts by groups to quickly access them. You access the groups you've created by tapping the Groups icon in the Dialer or the

Contacts app, as shown in Figure 3-29. You know where that leads; you can press the Menu button to send an email, create an invitation, and more.

FIGURE 3-29 You can view groups by tapping the Groups icon.

Using groups goes far beyond communicating through the Dialer or the Contacts app though; if you're in the Email app, you can simply type the name of the group to include every member in the To: line with a single tap. If you're in the Calendar app and create an event, you can opt to share that event via email or text, again, selecting the group to share with (versus individually typing each person's name).

To access your groups on the Droid X2 or the Droid 3, follow these steps:

1. Open the Contacts or Dialer app, and tap the Contacts tab if necessary.
2. Tap the Groups icon.
3. Tap any group in the list (refer to Figure 3-29).
4. To communicate with the entire group or to edit it, press the Menu button, and tap the appropriate option.

To access your groups on the Incredible 2, follow these steps:

1. Open the Phone or People app.
2. Press the Menu button, and then tap People if necessary.
3. Tap the Groups icon.
4. Tap any group in the list, as shown in Figure 3-30.

5. Communicate with the entire group by tapping the Send icon, as shown in Figure 3-31.

6. Tap Send Group Message or Send Group Mail to compose a message to the group.

FIGURE 3-30 Access your group by tapping the group in the Groups list.

FIGURE 3-31 Tap the Send icon to send a group message or a group email to the entire group.

To access your groups on the Droid Charge, follow these steps:

1. Open the Phone or Contacts app.

2. Tap the Contacts icon if necessary.

3. Tap the Groups icon.

4. Tap any group in the list, as shown in Figure 3-32.

5. Press the Menu button, and then tap Send Message or Send Email.

6. Tap the names you want to send a message to. See Figure 3-33.

7. Tap Send. Select the email account you want to use if necessary.

8. Compose your message, and send it to the selected members of your group.

FIGURE 3-32 Access your group by tapping the group in the Groups list.

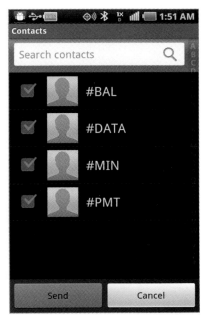

FIGURE 3-33 Check boxes appear next to the names you want to send a message to.

SHARING CONTACTS

You can share the contact information you have for any person with someone else through the Contacts or Dialer app. This enables you to send all of a contact's information without the need to copy and paste the data, or worse, type it.

There are lots of options for sharing data:

- ✚ **Bluetooth**—You can scan for nearby Bluetooth devices and choose available devices from a list.
- ✚ **Email**—You can email the information to any contact or email address.
- ✚ **Gmail**—You can email the information using Gmail.
- ✚ **Text Messaging**—You can send the information in a text message.
- ✚ **Others as applicable**—If you have third-party apps that can share data, you may see them listed. Figure 3-34 shows the V CAST Media Manager option.

When you're ready to share a contact's information, on the Droid 3 or the Droid X2:

1. Using any method, locate the contact and tap it.

2. Press the Menu button and tap Share.

3. Tap OK.

4. Select how to share: Bluetooth, Email, Gmail, or Text Messaging. Refer to Figure 3-34.

5. Locate the contact to share.

6. Complete as required; you may need to refer to other chapters of this book if you've never sent an email or text message.

FIGURE 3-34 You can share in many ways, including through third-party apps.

To share contact information on the Incredible 2, follow these steps:

1. Using any method, locate the contact.

2. Tap and hold the contact name until the Contact menu appears.

3. Tap Send Contact as vCard. The vCard file format is a standard for electronic business cards.

4. Select how you want to send the contact, as shown in Figure 3-35. You have four options: SMS, MMS, email, or Bluetooth.

5. Select the contact information that you want to include in the vCard. (You may need to scroll down.) By default, all contact information will be included.

6. Tap Send.

FIGURE 3-35 Select how you want to send information in the vCard by tapping Send Contact via SMS, which is the default option.

To share contact information on the Charge, follow these steps:

1. Using any method, locate the contact.

2. Tap and hold the contact name until the Contact menu appears.

3. Scroll down, and then tap Send Namecard Via.

4. Tap the sharing method by tapping Bluetooth, Email, or Gmail, as shown in Figure 3-36. If you want the method to be the default from now on, tap Use by Default for This Action.

5. Share the file by transferring the file via Bluetooth or attaching a vCard file to a Gmail or email message.

FIGURE 3-36 Tell the Contacts app that you want to complete the send action using Bluetooth, Email, or Gmail.

BE CAREFUL ABOUT SHARING CONTACT INFORMATION When you share a contact card through the Dialer or the Contact app (or using any other app as applicable), all the information on the card is shared, not just a person's email or phone number. Additionally, any notes you make about the person are sent as well, provided those notes are saved to the contact card. If you use the Contact app to keep sensitive information, it's best to find another way to share, so that information is not sent out to others.

JOINING CONTACTS

You may find, after using your phone for some time, that you have duplicate entries for a single contact, as shown in Figure 3-37, or that for whatever reason, two contacts need to be joined. (Perhaps two of your friends got married, and now they live in the same household.) You can join a contact from the

Edit Contact screen on the Droid X2 and the Droid 3. From the Charge and Incredible 2, you join the contacts (what the Incredible 2 calls linking) in the contact's information screen.

To join a contact with another contact on the Droid X2 or Droid 3, follow these steps:

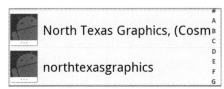

FIGURE 3-37 It's easy to acquire duplicate contacts and the Join command helps you control them.

1. Open the Contacts or Dialer app, and tap the Contacts tab if necessary.

2. Tap and hold the contact to join with another, and choose Edit Contact.

3. Press the Menu button, and tap Join, as shown in Figure 3-38.

4. Tap the contact to join this one with.

5. Type a new name and edit other information as applicable.

6. Tap Save.

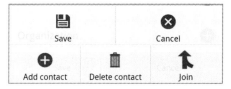

FIGURE 3-38 The Join option enables you to link two contacts together to become one.

To join a contact with another on the Droid Charge, follow these steps:

1. Open the Phone or Contacts app, and tap Contacts if necessary.

2. Tap the contact name in the list.

3. Scroll down the contact record (if necessary) until you see Join Contacts in the list, as shown in Figure 3-39.

4. Tap the number of joined contacts to view the list of contacts that your selected contact is joined with.

5. Tap Join Another Contact.

6. The Get Friends page suggests any potential contacts who can join with your selected contact, as shown in Figure 3-40.

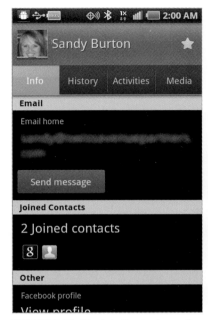

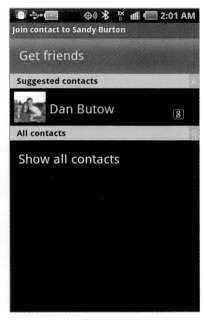

FIGURE 3-39 The Join Contacts section shows you how many other contacts your selected contact is joined with.

FIGURE 3-40 The Get Friends page suggests potential contacts who may be good matches based on those contacts' profiles.

7. Tap a suggested contact in the list, or tap All Contacts to view all your contacts and select one from the list.

8. The Joined Contacts page shows your new contact on the screen. You can join another contact or press Back to return to the Contact screen.

To join a contact with another on the Droid Incredible 2, follow these steps:

1. Open the Phone or People widget.

2. Press Menu, and tap People if necessary.

3. Tap the contact name in the list.

4. Tap Menu and then tap Link.

5. In the Linked Contacts screen, as shown in Figure 3-41, you can add contacts in your Contacts list or add contacts from Facebook and other social networking sites you're connected to in the Add Contact section. (You may need to scroll down to reach this section.)

6. Tap All Contacts.

7. Scroll down until you find the contact you want to link to and then tap the contact name.

8. The Linked Contacts screen shows the new linked contact at the top of the screen, as shown in Figure 3-42. Add another linked contact by tapping an option in the Add Contact section and then selecting a contact.

9. Tap Done to return to the contact screen. Go back to the All Contacts screen by pressing Back.

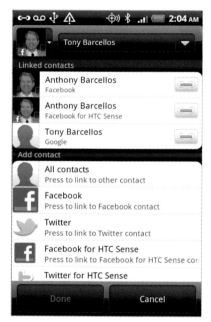

FIGURE 3-41 In the Linked Contacts page, you can see the contacts your selected contact is linked to, and you can also link to other contacts and social networking site profiles.

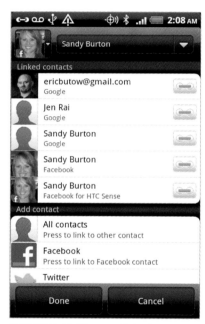

FIGURE 3-42 The new linked contact appears at the top of the contact screen.

DELETING CONTACTS To delete a contact, tap and hold it. Then, tap Delete Contact. You may need to tap OK to verify.

SYNCING CONTACTS

Syncing is what happens when you make changes to data on one device, and the changes appear on another. This syncing can be manual or automatic. Many people manually sync music to their Droid phone by connecting it (using a USB cable) to a PC, and then they use a syncing program to complete the sync. This keeps the same music on both devices, and purchases that have been made either at the PC or on the Droid phone are transferred to the other.

You can also sync your contacts. This is an important task if you keep contacts on multiple devices. Although there are many ways to keep contacts in sync, including using third-party software from the Market, the easiest way by far is to make sure that all your devices sync automatically to Google's servers, as outlined earlier in this chapter, syncing your Contacts with Google. That's because when you make changes to a contact that's associated with your Google account, those changes appear automatically on your other devices and computers. Because you already have a Google account, see if you can configure your other devices to also use it, and let Google handle the syncing, if you can.

When you're all-in with Google, you can configure sync settings on your Droid (and on your other devices). On the Droid X2 and the Droid, follow these steps:

1. Press the Menu button and tap Settings.

2. Tap Accounts.

3. Tap your Gmail (Google) account, as shown in Figure 3-43. (Later you can come back to your other accounts to see if syncing is an option for them.)

4. Choose what you want to sync. See Figure 3-44.

5. Press the Menu button and tap Sync Now.

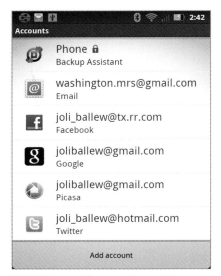

FIGURE 3-43 After a while, you'll have lots of accounts on your Droid phone, and some are capable of syncing.

FIGURE 3-44 You may want to sync only contacts, or you may want to sync everything you use with Google, including Books.

DON'T FORGET TO SET UP VOICEMAIL Voicemail was not covered in this chapter because the setup process is dependent on the carrier, not the phone or its manufacturer. For the most part, you need to follow the directions in the User's Manual that came with your phone, or tap the Voicemail icon on one of your Home screens. Alternatively, you can access the Voicemail icon on the Droid X2 and the Droid 3 from the All Apps page from your phone.

Related Questions

✦ What do the network icons mean? **PAGE 55**

✦ How do I sync music? **PAGE 62**

✦ How can I get contacts to Google's servers? **PAGE 56**

✦ Where can I find apps to help manage and sync my contacts? **PAGE 120**

✦ How do I use email? **PAGE 155**

CHAPTER FOUR

HOW DO I USE AND MANAGE THE WIRELESS AND CELLULAR FEATURES?

Your Droid comes with several wireless features and lots of ways to communicate with others. This chapter discusses four types of connections: connecting to the Internet via Wi-Fi networks, both open and secure; connecting to the Internet through subscription data services; sharing your Droid's mobile data connection by tethering it to a device using a USB cable; and sharing your Droid's mobile data connection with multiple devices by creating your own Wi-Fi hotspot.

Using Wireless Features

You can use Wi-Fi to connect to your own private Wi-Fi network or a public one. You can access free, public Wi-Fi hotspots in businesses, libraries, hotels, and coffee shops all over the country. When Wi-Fi isn't available either because you're not within range of a network or because you do not have permission to use it, you can connect using whatever cellular technology is available from where you are (such as CDMA, 3G or 4G, and applicable variations of these). Because Wi-Fi offers a way to connect to the Internet without going through your cellular provider's network satellites, cell towers, and other mobile infrastructures, it's free on your Droid. If a Wi-Fi network is available, there are a ton of reasons why you should opt for it whenever possible.

WI-FI ISN'T AVAILABLE EVERYWHERE Connecting with Wi-Fi requires you be in range of a local wireless network such as the one in your home or a local coffee shop, and that you know the log on credentials if any are required. Unsecured Wi-Fi isn't available everywhere though, and Wi-Fi administrators won't always give you permission to use their protected Wi-Fi networks.

First, Wi-Fi has the potential to be faster than 3G, and possibly even 4G. It's almost always faster than any type of CDMA connection. Of course, the speed you get depends on various factors, but most of the time, Wi-Fi *is* faster—period.

Second, when you connect to a wireless network, data you send and receive across the Internet isn't charged against your data plan. This means that while connected to a Wi-Fi network, you can upload and view videos to your heart's content; send and receive photos and videos; and even download music and media without worrying about how much data you send and receive.

Third, after you connect to a wireless network once, you'll automatically be connected the next time you're in range of it. Again, this helps minimize the data you send over your cellular network and improves performance; of course, it's also a nice convenience.

As you can see in Figure 4-1, you can configure several wireless and network settings. This is a Droid X2, and it's connected to a Wi-Fi network named 3802.

CONNECTING WITH WI-FI AND CONFIGURING ADDITIONAL WI-FI SETTINGS

FIGURE 4-1 You want to connect to Wi-Fi when possible.

Although Chapter 1 ("How Do I Get Started with Droid?") covered enabling Wi-Fi and joining your own Wi-Fi network, it is worth repeating here if you're skipping around, and there are other options you've yet to explore. If you recall, joining your own Wi-Fi network on the Droid X2 and the Droid 3, you need to follow these steps:

1. Press the Menu button and tap Settings.

2. Tap Wireless & Networks.

3. Tap Wi-Fi to connect to or disconnect from a Wi-Fi network. Refer to Figure 4-1.

4. If applicable, when connecting to a network, touch the network you want to connect to.

5. Type the passcode, password, or passphrase, if one is required.

6. Tap Done and Connect, as applicable.

Although connecting to an available network isn't particularly difficult, you can get hung up if you don't know the password or forget that passwords are case-sensitive. If necessary, ask someone what the password is, or if they can help you (especially in a public establishment).

To connect to a Wi-Fi network on the Droid Charge and Incredible 2, follow these steps:

1. Press Menu and then tap Settings.

2. Tap Wireless & Network or Wireless & Networks. If you have a Droid Incredible 2, skip to Step 4.

3. Tap Wi-Fi Settings.

4. Tap Wi-Fi to connect or disconnect from a Wi-Fi network.

5. Type the Network SSID; select the Security type and the wireless password if they are required.

6. Tap Save or Connect, as applicable. The Wi-Fi or Wi-Fi Settings screen show that you are connected to the network, as shown in Figure 4-2.

FIGURE 4-2 The Droid Charge is connected to the BCG Wi-Fi network.

Enabling and Disabling Network Notifications

You should leave Wi-Fi enabled and connect to Wi-Fi networks when they are available. However, you may not need your Droid to search for new networks all the time, especially if you use your Droid only (or mainly) at home or at work. In these cases, your Droid already knows the networks you connect to, and thus, there's no reason for your Droid to constantly search for others. Disabling notifications prevents the Droid from always looking for new networks and makes your battery last longer.

You can tell the Droid to notify you (or not) of available Wi-Fi networks when you're within range of them. Follow these steps on the Droid X2 and the Droid 3:

1. Press the Menu button and tap Settings.
2. Tap Wireless & Networks.
3. Tap Wi-Fi Settings.
4. Under Network notification:
   A. Tap the box beside Open Network to enable or disable notifications about unsecure networks.
   B. Tap the box beside Secure Network to enable or disable notifications about secure networks. See Figure 4-3.
5. Tap the Home button to return to the default Home screen.

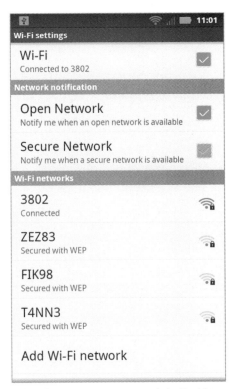

FIGURE 4-3 You may not need the Droid to search for and notify you of secure and open networks.

Follow these steps on the Droid Incredible 2 and the Droid Charge:

1. Press Menu and then tap Settings.

2. Tap Wireless & Networks (or Wireless & Network as applicable).

3. Tap Wi-Fi Settings.

4. The network notification check box is checked by default, as shown in Figure 4-4, which means the phone is actively searching for networks. If you want to disable this service, tap the check box.

5. Press Home to return to the default Home screen.

FIGURE 4-4 Tap the Network notification check box so that the Droid won't notify you of available new networks because the default setting is to notify you of such networks.

Managing Your Network List

You can save a little more battery power by removing networks from the network list that you've connected to before, but know you'll never use again. When you forget a network, the Droid will no longer look for it. You'll find that over time this list can get long, especially if you travel or visit lots of places that offer free Wi-Fi.

To "forget" a network from the Droid X2 and the Droid 3, follow these steps:

1. Press the Menu button and tap Settings.

2. Tap Wireless & Networks.

3. Tap Wi-Fi Settings.

4. Tap Manage Networks.

5. Tap the network to forget, in this case, James. See Figure 4-5.

6. Tap Forget.

FIGURE 4-5 Remove unwanted networks to keep your Droid from constantly looking for them.

To "forget" a network from the Droid Incredible 2 and Droid Charge, follow these steps:

1. Press Menu and then tap Settings.
2. Tap Wireless & Networks (or Wireless & Network, as applicable).
3. Tap Wi-Fi Settings.
4. Tap the network you're connected to, in this case, BCG.
5. Tap Forget or Disconnect, as applicable.

- -

WHAT ABOUT GPS? A Global Positioning System (GPS) is also a kind of wireless technology. With it, your Droid can be configured to triangulate your position through satellite signals and Wi-Fi networks. Maps uses GPS, as do other apps, but you can't use it to connect to any particular network, so it won't be discussed here.

- -

LEARNING ABOUT PUBLIC WI-FI HOTSPOTS

A free, public mobile hotspot is often a perk offered by a hotel, coffee shop, pub, and the like, where you can go and connect to the Internet for free. These hotspots are generally unsecured, meaning they don't require you type in a password. Thus, to connect, all you need to do is tap the network and tap Connect, as applicable to your phone. On most phones, you can access these networks by pulling down on the Status bar.

Keep in mind that open, public networks are not secure and may open your Droid up to eavesdropping; and a skilled hacker might intercept your keystrokes. (Although it's unlikely, it's still something to consider.) It's a good idea to avoid entering sensitive data while on an open network, and to cover your keyboard with a free hand when you must type a password, credit card number, or Social Security number. (Although it's best to do any of that only on a protected network.)

EXPLORE NETWORKING WIDGETS The Motorola Droid 2 comes with several networking widgets. There is an Airplane mode toggle, a GPS toggle, and a Wi-Fi toggle, for instance. These widgets appear on the screen and enable you to turn on or off these networking features with a single tap. The Droid 3 offers a few of these as well as similar widgets, including a Data Usage widget that can come in handy if you need to monitor your data usage over a cellular network. (To add these widgets, press the Menu button, and tap Add. Choose Motorola widgets, Android widgets, or widgets, as applicable to your phone.)

FINDING AND CONNECTING TO FREE WI-FI HOTSPOTS

You can find Wi-Fi hotspots in many ways. You can search for them on the Internet using the Browser app by typing something such as **free Wi-Fi hotspots** followed by your zip code; you can ask friends where they connect or proprietors of businesses if they offer free Wi-Fi; and you can leave notifications enabled on your Droid and check the Status bar when you think a free Wi-Fi network is nearby. When you're within range, it's easy to connect.

If you've left notifications regarding open networks enabled on your Droid, you'll see a Wi-Fi notification on your phone's Status bar when an open Wi-Fi network is available. You can tap, drag, and pull down on the Status bar to see information about the network and then tap it to join. You learned how to do this in Chapter 1.

If you don't see a network you think you should see and nothing appears in the drop-down area of the Status bar, on the Droid X2 and Droid 3, follow these steps:

1. Press the Menu button and tap Settings.

2. Tap Wireless & Networks.

3. Tap Wi-Fi Settings.

4. Tap the network to join. Tap Connect, as shown in Figure 4-6.

FIGURE 4-6 When a network is open, you won't need to type a password.

5. If you don't see the network listed, either in the Status bar pull-down or the Wi-Fi networks list, follow these steps:

   A. Tap Add Wi-Fi Network.

   B. Type the name of the network. See Figure 4-7.

   C. Leave Open selected.

   D. Tap Save.

To connect to a free Wi-Fi hotspot on a Charge or Incredible 2, follow these steps:

1. Press Menu and then tap Settings.

2. Tap Wireless & Networks (or Wireless & Network if applicable). If you're using a Droid Incredible 2, skip to Step 4.

3. Tap Wi-Fi Settings.

4. Tap Wi-Fi. If you use a Droid Charge, skip to Step 6.

5. Tap Wi-Fi Settings.

6. The Droid automatically searches for available networks both locked and open.

7. Tap the network you want to connect to. Tap Yes if applicable.

8. Tap the Password in the Key or Wireless password box, and then tap Connect. If the Wi-Fi network is open, you won't see this screen because an open network doesn't require a password.

9. The Droid obtains the IP address of the network and reports that it's connected. A Wi-Fi icon appears in the status bar, as shown in Figure 4-8, to indicate that you're connected.

FIGURE 4-7 You'll rarely need to add a network manually, but you can.

FIGURE 4-8 The Wi-Fi icon in the status bar indicates that you have a functioning Wi-Fi network connection.

Understanding Cellular Features

You will generally connect to only two types of network: Wi-Fi or cellular. When you're connected to Wi-Fi, you can surf the Internet without using any data from your data plan. When you're not connected to Wi-Fi, you'll be connected to the Internet through your cellular provider's network.

The type of network you use (when Wi-Fi isn't available) depends on your phone, the provider, the type of network that's available, and other factors. For example, although you may have a 4G compatible phone, you can connect using 4G only if you're in a 4G area and your provider offers the service. Likewise, you can connect with 3G only when you're in a 3G service area. If you can't connect to 4G or 3G, another network type will be accessed. You can find out how you're connected from your phone's Status bar. In Figure 4-9, that's 3G.

FIGURE 4-9 The Status bar offers information about the type of network you're connected to.

When you make phone calls with your phone, you use your provider's network. You can obtain information about that network from your Droid's About Phone option. To see the network information, including the signal strength, mobile network type, and service state, on the Droid X2 and the Droid 3, follow these steps:

1. Press the Menu button and tap Settings.

2. Tap About Phone. You may need to scroll down.

3. Tap Status.

4. Note what's shown under Network, Mobile Network Type, Service State, Roaming, and Mobile Network State. See Figure 4-10.

Although there isn't much you can do with this information, meaning you can't tap say, Network, and choose a different one, or tap Roaming and enable or disable roaming,

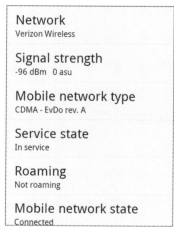

Network
Verizon Wireless

Signal strength
-96 dBm 0 asu

Mobile network type
CDMA - EvDo rev. A

Service state
In service

Roaming
Not roaming

Mobile network state
Connected

FIGURE 4-10 You can find information about your networks from About Phone ⇨ Status.

you can at least learn how you're connected at any given moment and talk to technicians if problems arise.

To find this information on the Charge or Incredible 2, follow these steps:

1. Press Menu and then tap Settings.

2. Scroll down to the bottom of the list and then tap About Phone. If you're using a Droid Incredible 2, skip to Step 4.

3. Tap Status. Scroll down the list to view the Network status, Signal Strength, Mobile Network Type, Service State, Roaming status, and Mobile Network State.

4. Tap Network. Note what's shown under Network, including the Operator Name, Signal Strength, Mobile Network Type, Service State, and Roaming status. See Figure 4-11.

FIGURE 4-11 Information about your network on the Droid Incredible 2.

Finally, some Droid devices (generally tablets) enable you to turn off Wi-Fi, turn on Cellular, or turn off both when they aren't needed. Most of the Droid phones do enable you to turn off Wi-Fi but don't offer an option for cellular. The only way to turn off cellular features is to enable Airplane Mode. You learn about that at the end of the chapter. For the most part, you want cellular enabled.

Sharing Your Droid's Mobile Data Connection

You may have noticed while exploring the Wireless & Network(s) options on your Droid X2, Droid 3, or Droid Charge that there are two additional options related to networks: Tethering & Mobile Hotspot (called Tethering on the Charge) and VPN settings. The Droid Incredible 2 enables you to set up a 3G Mobile Hotspot and VPN settings as well.

WHAT IS TETHERING, AND WHAT ARE HOTSPOTS?

Tethering is a way to share your Droid's Internet connection with another device, such as a laptop or netbook, by physically connecting it with a USB cable. The cable is supplied and ships with your Droid. You must use the cable to tether; therefore, you can tether only one device at a time. The device you want to tether must have an available USB port.

Setting up and using a Wi-Fi hotspot through the Droid is another way to share your Droid's Internet connection; however, you do not need to connect the secondary device with a USB cable; hotspots are wireless. Because no cable is required, you can connect more than one device at a time to your personal hotspot, and you can connect devices that don't have a USB port.

Whatever data your laptop or netbook (or other compatible device) uses while connected in either manner counts against your data plan and toward your monthly usage totals. Additionally, for both scenarios, you must enable the proper options in the Wireless & Networks Settings before it can work. It is not enabled by default. And there's one more important requirement: All applicable drivers must be installed on the computer you want to tether or connect to configure a successful connection.

SETTING UP TETHERING

When you connect a new device to a Windows computer, the computer attempts to install the device driver for it. A device driver enables two devices to communicate with each other. If the device is new, such as a Droid X2 or Droid 3, the computer probably must get the required drivers from the Internet. It does this with its own built-in update software. For the most part, you simply need to wait for this to happen, as shown in Figure 4-12.

FIGURE 4-12 On Windows PCs, drivers for your Droid phone might install automatically.

Sometimes, a computer can't find a driver though, as was the case with our Droid Incredible 2. If this happens to you, you'll have to find the driver and install it. To do this, visit the manufacturer's support pages, perhaps starting at the Motorola Support page, and then moving on to the Verizon Wireless Support page. You may also have to search for a solution. Consider a query such as **Download Droid Incredible 2 Driver**. After you find the driver, download and install it.

SET UP TETHERING BEFORE YOU NEED TO TETHER Because several drivers need to be installed before you can successfully tether your Droid to a secondary device such as a netbook or laptop, you need to set up tethering when the secondary device is already connected to the Internet using some other method so that, if required, drivers can be obtained from the Internet through the computer's update software.

Also be sure that USB storage is turned off on your Droid phone. If you have USB storage on, which means that your computer can see your Droid as another hard drive, it supersedes all other functions that use a USB connection. You can check by pulling down the Status bar and finding out if you have an option to turn off USB storage in the Notification menu.

After your Droid is connected and drivers have been successfully installed, you're ready to tether. Remember, any data usage on the laptop or netbook is charged against the Droid's data plan.

To set up tethering and connect with a secondary mobile device such as a laptop on the Droid X2 and Droid 3, follow these steps:

1. Connect your phone to the device you'd like to tether using the supplied USB cable.

2. From the Droid X2 or Droid 3:

   A. Tap the Menu icon.

   B. Tap Settings.

   C. Tap Wireless & Networks.

   D. Tap Tethering & Mobile Hotspot.

   E. Tap USB Tethering to place a check in it. By default it will not be checked, as shown in Figure 4-13.

FIGURE 4-13 You must enable tethering; as you can see here, it's not enabled by default.

3. It may be necessary for the drivers to install again. If so, wait until it completes.

4. Choose Public if prompted for a network type, at least the first time you connect. Later you can experiment with another type if you want.

5. Note the connection in any network window; Figure 4-14 shows what the Network and Sharing Center on a Windows 7 netbook display.

6. When you no longer need to tether, disconnect the device. Also, disable the tethering option on the Droid phone.

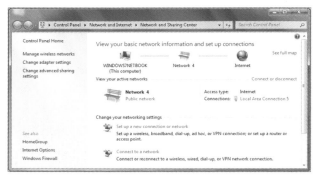

FIGURE 4-14 When tethering is enabled, you have access to the Internet from your secondary device.

To set up tethering and connect with a secondary mobile device such as a laptop, on the Charge, follow these steps:

1. Press Menu and then tap Settings.

2. Tap Wireless & Networks (or Wireless & Network if applicable).

3. Tap Tethering, as shown in Figure 4-15.

4. It may be necessary for the drivers to install again. If so, wait until they completes.

5. Choose Public if you're prompted for a network type; this happens at least

FIGURE 4-15 Activate USB tethering by tapping Tethering in the list.

the first time you connect. Later you can experiment with another type if wanted.

6. Note the connection in any network window; refer to Figure 4-14.

7. When you no longer need to tether, disconnect the device. Also, disable the tethering option on the Droid phone.

SETTING UP A WI-FI HOTSPOT

If you want to use your Droid as a Wi-Fi hotspot with a computer such as a laptop or netbook, you must perform some of the same tasks as you performed before tethering. Specifically, you must have already installed the required USB drivers on the computer you want to use. If you haven't done this yet, refer to the previous sections that introduce tethering to learn how. After that, you simply enable the Mobile Hotspot feature on your phone and connect with your laptop or netbook.

To set up a Wi-Fi mobile hotspot on the Droid X2 or Droid 3, follow these steps:

1. Tap the Menu button.

2. Tap Settings.

3. Tap Wireless & Networks.

4. Tap Tethering & Mobile Hotspot.

5. Tap Mobile Hotspot, and tap OK in the warning box.

6. Tap Configure Mobile Hotspot.

7. Note the information offered. An example is shown in Figure 4-16. You may have to tap Show Password.

8. From the laptop, netbook, or other device, select the available wireless network connections.

FIGURE 4-16 Mobile hotspots are wireless and secure.

Figure 4-17 shows how it appears on a Windows 7 netbook.

9. Click Connect or other applicable option.

10. Type the security key, and click OK, as applicable to your device.

11. Complete any additional tasks as required by your secondary device.

12. Most of the time, as shown in Figure 4-18, you'll be prompted that the new network was successfully created.

FIGURE 4-17 How you connect to a Wi-Fi hotspot differs depending on the device you use to connect.

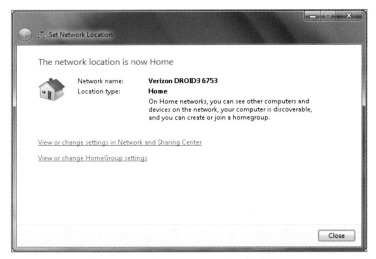

FIGURE 4-18 When connected to your Droid's mobile hotspot, you can access the Internet from the secondary device.

To set up a mobile hotspot on the Charge, follow these steps:

1. Tap Applications.

2. Tap Mobile Hotspot.

3. Tap Network Settings in the Mobile Hotspot screen.

4. Tap Configure and then tap Yes.

5. Tap Manual to review the Droid mobile hotspot information that the Mobile Hotspot app will set up automatically, as shown in Figure 4-19.

6. Tap Done. If Wi-Fi is on, tap Turn Wi-Fi Off.

7. Tap Mobile Hotspot to turn the hotspot on. You can then tap Network Settings to manage your settings, and as many as 10 people can connect to the Internet through your mobile hotspot via Wi-Fi.

To set up a Wi-Fi mobile hotspot on the Incredible 2, follow these steps:

1. Tap Apps in the Dock.

2. Tap 3G Mobile Hotspot.

3. The app adds mobile hotspot information automatically in the Settings section, as shown in Figure 4-20. You can change these settings if you want.

4. Tap 3G Mobile Hotspot at the top of the screen.

5. The Status bar notes that the mobile hotspot is active and places a red icon in the Status bar.

6. Follow the instructions on the screen, and then tap OK. You return to the Settings window, so you can manage as many as five connections to your 3G Mobile Hotspot using Wi-Fi.

FIGURE 4-19 The Mobile Hotspot app adds default information into the account, but you can change this if you want.

FIGURE 4-20 The Settings section contains the router name, security protocol, and access password.

WHY DON'T THE DROID CHARGE AND INCREDIBLE 2 USE WI-FI INSTEAD OF THEIR OWN PAY-TO-PLAY MOBILE HOTSPOT SERVICE? You probably noticed that you get only a brief trial period with the Mobile Hotspot Service on both the Droid Charge and Droid Incredible 2. Verizon wants to find out how much interest it can generate from a mobile hotspot service with 3G and 4G speeds than take the time to create a Wi-Fi mobile hotspot service as the Droid X2 and Droid 3 have. At the time of this writing, it is unclear whether Verizon will ever create a Wi-Fi mobile hotspot service for the Charge and Incredible 2.

And finally, if you want to connect to the Wi-Fi hotspot from a device that is not a laptop, netbook, or computer, but is instead a phone, smartphone, or tablet with Wi-Fi capabilities, you need to connect to the network in whatever manner you've used previously to connect to Wi-Fi hotspots. If your device can't connect to Wi-Fi hotspots, you cannot connect to one you create with your Droid phone.

BE SURE TO DISABLE THE TETHERING AND MOBILE HOTSPOT FEATURE WHEN YOU FINISH USING IT! When you no longer need to provide tethering or a mobile hotspot from your Droid, disable the feature. If you forget, a netbook or laptop could remain connected for a long time and use quite a bit of data without your knowledge. Additionally, if you opt to connect a device to your Droid's hotspot automatically, a computer could connect on its own if the two are within range.

Using Airplane Mode

It's likely that at some time in your life you've heard a captain on an airplane say that all wireless devices must be turned off and stowed. You probably also heard her say it's OK to use approved devices as long as you disable any wireless features when you're up in the air (and properly reclined in your seat). That's where Airplane Mode comes in. With Airplane Mode you can play games, watch media stored on your phone, view items in your Gallery, view files, and perform other non-Internet or non–phone-call related tasks, all while sitting on an airplane.

To enable or disable Airplane Mode, follow these steps:

1. Press the Menu button and tap Settings.

2. Tap Wireless & Networks.

3. Tap Airplane mode. See Figure 4-21.

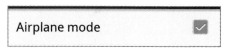

FIGURE 4-21 Airplane Mode disables all wireless features.

If you travel a lot, consider putting a shortcut to Airplane Mode on your Home screen. This can enable you to get to Airplane mode with a single tap. Almost any phone offers this as an option, and there are plenty of third-party apps that also do. Figure 4-22 is an example from the Motorola Droid X2. It's a widget that can be added called Airplane Mode Toggle.

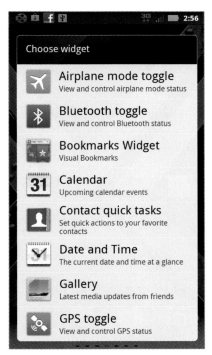

FIGURE 4-22 Add an Airplane Mode Toggle widget if your phone offers one.

I DON'T SEE THE POINT OF USING AIRPLANE MODE WHILE ON A PLANE. WHO'S GOING TO KNOW, AND WHAT HARM COULD IT CAUSE? You're not the only one to feel like this or question the usefulness. However, it's best to play by the rules. The FCC's main concern (and it's a valid one) is that cell phones may interfere with the communication and navigational systems on the plane. This could cause disruptions in cabin pressure, problems with compass function, and cause various other system failures. In fact, numerous airlines have reported disruptions they attribute to cell phone interference. They're not just making it up; it's best to follow the rules.

Related Questions

✛ How do I connect to my company's virtual private network? **ONLINE AT** www.wiley.com/go/droidcompanion

✛ How do I connect a Bluetooth device? **PAGE 30**

✛ How do I send a text? **PAGE 140**

✛ How do I find apps that I can use to manage my network settings? **PAGE 120**

CHAPTER FIVE

HOW DO I GET THE MOST FROM THE ANDROID MARKET?

In This Chapter:

+ Getting Familiar with the Market's Interface

+ Obtaining and Using Apps

+ Managing Apps

+ Exploring Games, Books, and Movies

The Market app, available from virtually any Droid's Home screen enables you to access the Market with a single tap. The Market icon is shown in Figure 5-1. (If you've moved the Market app, look in the All Apps page.) The Market is an online store where you can browse, buy, and download media including apps, games, books, and movies. The Market's interface makes it easy to find what you want; you can search by app name, book, and movie title; by developer name; by actor, actress, or author; by what's most popular; by what's free; by what's featured; and more. The Market also enables you to rate, suggest, and comment on apps and books after you purchase them, among other things.

FIGURE 5-1
The Market icon looks like a shopping bag.

Getting Familiar with the Market's Interface

As you can see in Figure 5-2, the Market on the Droid X2, Droid 3, and Droid Charge is separated into sections. There are Apps, Games, Books, and Movies on the left, and popular items on the right. You can scroll down to see more items. The Droid Incredible 2 looks a little different, offering only Apps and Games from its screen, which you see shortly.

Each time you tap an option on the Home page of the Market, a back arrow and title bar appear across the top. Figure 5-3 shows how this looks on the Droid X2, Droid 3, and Droid Charge. (Figure 5-5 shows how the Market appears on the Incredible 2.) Tap the back arrow or the shopping bag icon that's next to it to go back a page. (On many phones, you can also tap the Back button on the phone itself.) This helps you navigate

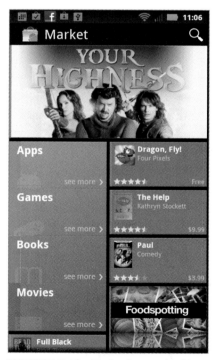

FIGURE 5-2 The Market is organized in sections and offers quick access to what's currently hot.

the Market in the same manner as you would a website. You can also tap the title bar, in this case, Games, to return to the previous screen, but this doesn't always work. Finally, you can press the Back button on the phone to return to the previous Market page.

Back button

FIGURE 5-3 After you "drill into" the Market, you can see an arrow and a title bar that enables you to return to the previous page.

To learn to navigate the Market on the Droid X2, Droid 3, and Droid Charge, work through these steps:

1. From a Home screen or the All Apps page, tap the Market icon.

2. If you are not on the Market main screen, use the arrow shown earlier in Figure 5-3 to get there. Tap Movies.

3. Tap any movie to see its description.

4. If wanted, scroll through and read the offered information.

5. Tap the title bar to return to the previous screen. (If that doesn't work, tap the back arrow or the Back button on your phone.) If applicable, tap again to return to the screen shown in Figure 5-2.

6. Repeat with Apps, Games, and Books.

FIGURE 5-4 You may get a preview of what you're considering buying or downloading.

7. As shown in Figure 5-4, you can often get a free sample of a book, and in other areas, see an app in action or get a preview of a movie.

DIFFERENCES WITH THE DROID AND THE MARKET, OUTSIDE THE UNITED STATES What you see in the Market and on your Droid if you purchased it somewhere other than the United States (where this book was written and published) may not be exactly what is shown here.

To navigate the Market on the Droid Incredible 2:

1. On the Home screen, tap the Market icon.

2. In the Market home screen, as shown in Figure 5-5, scroll through the Featured list.

3. Tap a featured app in the list to view it and, if wanted, scroll through to read information about the app.

4. Press Back to return to the Market home page.

5. Tap Apps to view a list of categories that you can browse. See Figure 5-6.

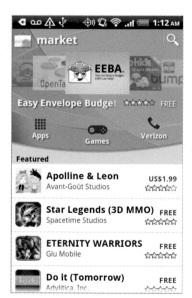

FIGURE 5-5 Check out the Incredible Market home screen.

FIGURE 5-6 There are several Apps categories..

6. In the Top paid screen, tap a category to view a list of apps available for you to buy.

7. Press Back to return to the Apps page. Repeat steps 6 and 7 for different categories such as Medical and Shopping.

8. As when you browse the Market on other Droid models, you can often get a free sample of a book, and in other areas, see an app in action, or get a preview of a movie. Refer to Figure 5-4 for an example.

As you explore the various sections of the Market, you see how those sections are organized. For instance, if you tap Apps on the Droid X2, Droid 3, or Droid Charge, you see, across the top of the screen, Categories, Featured, and Top Paid, but others are available you can't see: Top Free, Top Grossing, Top New Paid, Top New Free, and Trending.

To get to these sections, flick left and right on the screen. As you flick, the entire screen moves in the direction you flick, and the items under the title bar change to offer additional options. Figure 5-7 shows the dragging technique in action, and here you can see more options, including Top Grossing and Top New Paid.

If you tap Apps within the Market on the Incredible 2 and then tap an application category, you see three categories across the top of the screen, as shown in Figure 5-8: Top Paid, Top Free, and Just In. As with any other model, you simply tap the item to enter into the category.

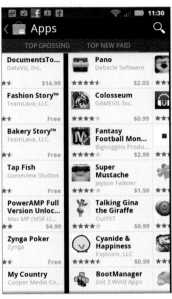

FIGURE 5-7 While in the Apps section of the Market, flick left and right to see additional screens.

FIGURE 5-8 The Top Paid, Top Free, and Just In categories appear on the All applications screen.

WHY FOCUS ON APPS? In the previous section and the next, you learn how to find, choose, buy, download, and use apps. After you know how to do that, you can apply those same principles to choosing, buying (or renting), and downloading other types of media including games, movies, and books.

Obtaining and Using Apps

Apps are programs you can run on your Droid phone, generally to help you perform tasks, acquire information, or calculate data. You can compare Droid apps to apps on an iPhone, widgets on a Mac, or gadgets on a PC, if you're familiar with any of those. You probably have lots of apps on your phone:

+ **Books**—Read e-books you acquire.
+ **Calculator**—Perform calculations.
+ **Calendar**—Create and manage important dates and events.
+ **Email and Gmail**—Read, send, and manage email.
+ **Google Search**—Find information on the web by typing or by voice search.
+ **Maps**—Find a location or map a route.
+ **Talk**—Communicate with other Talk users.
+ **YouTube**—View movies and videos.

As you can gather from this list, apps help you do things. You can explore thousands of apps available from the Market. As you know, to browse apps, you enter the Market and tap Apps on any Droid phone. You can then cull the list until you find something interesting, by choosing a category or flicking to an appropriate screen (such as Top Free).

HELP! I'M LOST IN THE MARKET! If you're lost in the Market and can't find your way to the Home page, tap the Market icon in the top-left corner. If you're really lost, you may have to tap it once more.

LEARNING MORE ABOUT ANY APP

You can learn more about any app by tapping its icon. This opens the Details page. You can find lots of information, including the price of the app (if it isn't free), the option to download it, a description of the app, and more. You can even tap More in many Details pages to expand on what is already shown. You can also read the description to ensure the app meets your needs.

You can also scroll down to learn more about the developer of the app and visit the developer's website. If you find that you recognize the developer, such as Google, and that it has high ratings and has been downloaded thousands of times, you can bet it's a stable and trusted app. You can use all this information to help you decide if you should get the app or continue searching. See Figure 5-9.

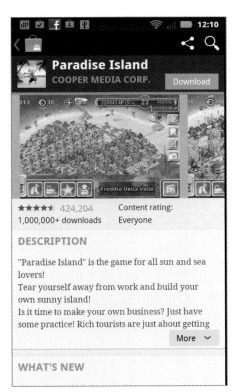

FIGURE 5-9 The Details page for an app offers lots of information about it.

WHAT YOU SEE ON YOUR DETAILS PAGE MAY DIFFER FROM WHAT YOU SEE HERE An app's Details page at the top may offer something other than the price and the option to download it. If you already have the app, for instance, it offers an Open icon. You can tap this to open the app. If an update is available, you see an Update icon. In addition, after you tap the price of an app, the icon changes to Accept & Buy. You can see more options while browsing and searching for movies, books, and the like that apply only to those items (such as *Rent*).

PAYING FOR, DOWNLOADING, AND INSTALLING AN APP

After you're convinced an app is right for you, you can purchase, download, and install it. (Purchasing won't be part of the process if you decide on a free app.) The steps are simple and are the same every time:

1. From your Droid phone, tap Market.

2. Locate an app to purchase or download.

3. If it's a free app, Tap Download; if it's a paid app:

   A. Tap the Price icon for the app, and then tap OK to accept permissions if necessary.

   B. Tap Accept & Buy, as shown in Figure 5-10. On the Incredible 2, tap Buy Now at the bottom of the screen.

4. If you've never purchased an app before or if you've yet to set up Google Checkout, you'll be prompted to enter payment information. Complete any steps required.

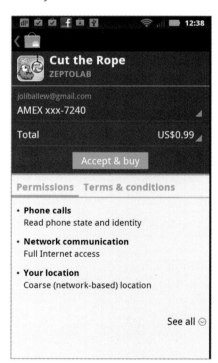

FIGURE 5-10 You must agree to the terms and conditions before you can buy the app.

5. Wait while the app downloads and installs, which requires no input from you. Watch the Status bar for download updates.

6. Tap Open.

7. If the app requires special permissions to run, you have to tap OK to allow the app to have these permissions. For the most part, this is generally OK to do. If you decide you don't want to allow these permissions, the app won't run. (You may want to uninstall and get a refund for the app if this is the case.)

8. Tap Accept to accept any terms of use or license agreements, if prompted.

- -

WHAT IF I DON'T LIKE AN APP OR IT DOESN'T WORK PROPERLY?
You have 15 minutes from the time you download an app to return it for a full refund. You may return a given application only once; if you purchase the same app again, you may not return it a second time.

To return an app, follow these steps:

1. From your Droid, tap Market.

2. Tap the Menu button, and tap My Apps.

3. Tap the app to return.

4. Tap Refund. (After 15 minutes, you'll see only Uninstall.)

5. If longer than 15 minutes has passed, you may still get a refund if you contact the developer directly, but there are no guarantees.

- -

MAKING APP PURCHASES FROM A COMPUTER

It may surprise you to know that you can browse the Market from any Internet-enabled device, and whatever you purchase automatically syncs to your Droid and will be available the next time you use it. Just browse to `http://market.android.com/`. Input your login credentials, browse as usual, and buy as usual. You can also see all your apps here, under My Library, as shown in Figure 5-11.

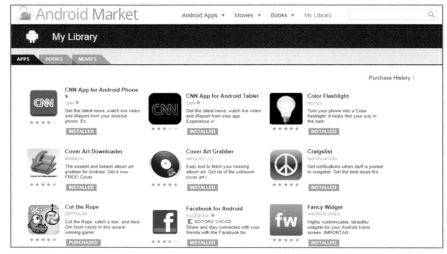

FIGURE 5-11 You can review and manage your apps, and even purchase apps, using your home computer.

If you do prefer to surf for apps on a computer, and if you have more than one Android device, you'll be prompted to choose the device to download the app to during the purchasing process. Figure 5-12 shows an example.

BE AWARE OF HOW MANY FREE APPS YOU ACQUIRE Your Droid comes with a specific amount of built-in storage, and you can add more to most Droid phones with a microSD card. This doesn't mean you should install every free app you run across without worry, though. You can run out of storage space, but more important, you can gunk up your Droid with *too* much stuff, making it difficult to find what you want when you want it.

FIGURE 5-12 If you have more than one Droid device, you must choose the device.

LEARNING HOW TO USE AN APP

The first time you use an app, you might see an introductory screen that offers instructions for using it. If you see instructions, read them! By reading the directions you can get much more from the app in both the short term and the long term.

If you don't receive any instructions when you first open the app or if you need more instruction later, you may obtain help from a Settings icon on the app's screen. You can tap and hold an empty area of the app's screen to access a menu, as shown in Figure 5-13 for Amazon's Kindle. Finally, you can try pressing the Menu button on your phone to see if help is available there.

You can also search the web for help with an app. Generally, a search using the app's name followed by the word **help**, **instructions**, or **directions** can produce useful results. You can also type **How to Play** or **How to Use**, followed by the app's name.

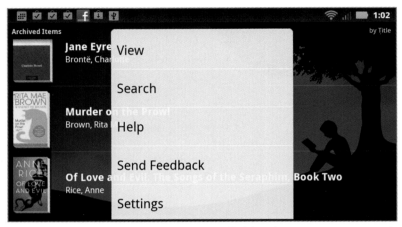

FIGURE 5-13 With some apps, you can tap and hold on the screen to access a Help option.

Managing Apps

You need to manage the apps you obtain, at least to get updates and to uninstall apps you don't like or use. Updates can resolve problems with apps you use, and uninstalling apps you don't like can help you keep your Droid from getting cluttered with unnecessary data, so both are important tasks.

UPDATING APPS

Manufacturers often offer updates to their apps to add features, enhance quality, or add additional data. When an update for an app you own or have down-loaded is available, you receive a notifi-cation on the Status bar on your Droid. This tiny icon looks like a briefcase with a down-facing arrow on it. Drag down on the Status bar to see the full notification as shown in Figure 5-14. You can tap that

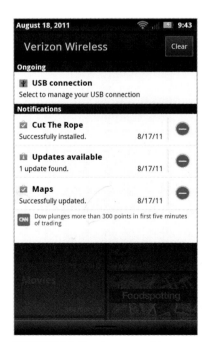

FIGURE 5-14 Developers provide updates to fix problems and add features.

notification to open the Market app to view information about the update and install it.

You can also manually check for updates. While in the Market, press the Menu button, and tap My Apps. Updated apps have Update listed next to them, as shown in Figure 5-15. To check for and review update information, and install app updates, follow these steps:

1. Tap the notification for the update on the Status bar or:

   A. Tap Market.

   B. Tap the Menu button.

   C. Tap My Apps.

   C. Tap the app to update. Refer to Figure 5-15 to see a YouTube update.

2. Scroll down to read the available information.

3. Tap Update or Allow Automatic Updating, and then tap Update. See Figure 5-16.

4. Tap Accept & Download.

HIDING AND UNINSTALLING APPS

Although this was detailed in Chapter 2 ("How Do I Make the Droid Uniquely Mine?"), it is worth repeating here: To remove an app shortcut from any screen on the Droid X2 and Droid 3, tap, hold, and drag the icon to the Trash icon that appears at the top of your Droid's screen. On the Droid Charge and Droid Incredible 2, tap,

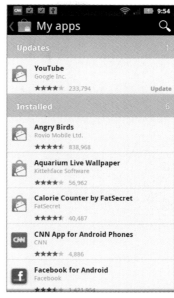

FIGURE 5-15 If Update is listed beside an app in the My Apps list, it has an update available.

FIGURE 5-16 If you trust future updates from this developer for this app, enable Allow Automatic Updating.

hold, and drag the icon to the Remove icon at the bottom of your Droid's screen. This hides the app's icon, but it is still available from the All Apps screen.

To uninstall an app and remove it completely from your Droid (which is different from simply removing it from a screen), follow these steps on the Droid X2 and the Droid 3:

1. Tap the Open Apps icon.

2. Tap All Apps, if it is showing, and tap Downloaded. See Figure 5-17.

3. Tap and hold the app to uninstall, and tap Uninstall when it appears.

4. Tap OK, and tap OK again when uninstall completes.

To completely uninstall an app on the Charge and Incredible 2, follow these steps:

1. Press Menu, and then tap Settings.

2. Tap Applications. (You may need to scroll down to find this option.)

3. Tap Manage Applications. The list of downloaded apps (called third-party apps by the Droid Charge) appears in the list.

4. Scroll to the app you want to delete if necessary, and then tap the app name.

5. Tap Uninstall, as shown in Figure 5-18.

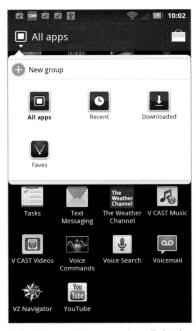

FIGURE 5-17 You can uninstall third-party apps.

FIGURE 5-18 Tap Uninstall to delete the app from your Droid.

Exploring Games, Books, and Movies

On the four phones detailed in this book you can browse for, download, and purchase apps and games from the default Market interface. On the Droid X2, Droid 3, and Droid Charge, you can also obtain books and movies in the same manner and from the same screen. Figure 5-19 shows the Market for the latter three phones.

The Market for the Droid Incredible 2 looks a little different and does not offer immediate access to books and movies. Figure 5-20 shows the Market for the Droid Incredible 2. On this phone, you need to tap Apps first, and then tap either Books & Reference or Media & Video in the list.

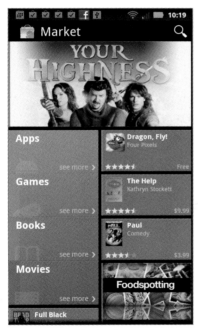

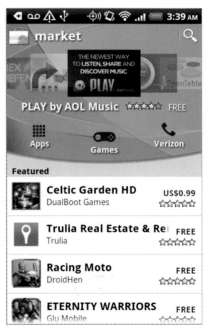

FIGURE 5-19 The Market as shown on this Droid 3 offers Apps, Games, Books, and Movies sections.

FIGURE 5-20 The Market on the Droid Incredible 2 offers Apps, Games, and Verizon sections.

DOWNLOADING AND PLAYING A GAME

To download and learn to play a game on any phone, open the Market and tap Games. Use what you've learned so far to browse the available games, including flicking left and right and viewing categories such as Top Paid, Top Free, and Categories.

When you find a game you like, follow these steps:

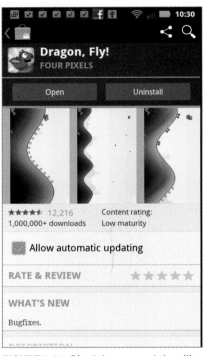

FIGURE 5-21 Obtaining games is just like obtaining apps.

1. Tap the game in the Market.

2. Tap either the price, Download, or Free as applicable.

3. Tap OK to accept permissions if applicable.

4. Tap Accept & Buy or Buy Now, as applicable.

5. Wait while the game downloads and installs, and then tap Open. See Figure 5-21.

6. Read any introductory information, and then tap Play.

WHAT GAME SHOULD I CHOOSE IF I'VE NEVER PLAYED A GAME?
You may have never played a game on your phone and are a bit stymied about where to start. If this is the case, flick to Top Free, and try Angry Birds, 3D Bowling, or Solitaire. These are intuitive and easy to learn and as you become more skilled, they can also challenge you.

DOWNLOADING AND READING A BOOK

The Books section of the Market is similar to the Apps section. The Books section offers categories across the top named Categories (to cull the list by Fiction, History, Humor, and so on), Featured, Top Selling, Top Free, and New

Arrivals. As with the Apps section, you browse these areas to locate a book you want, and then tap the book to buy it.

As you can surmise from the titles across the top, you can also download free books. This is a great place to start with books because you can get a free book, download it, and then learn how and where to read it. Figure 5-22 shows the Top Free section of the Books app as it appears on a Droid 3.

To obtain and read a free book, follow these steps:

1. Tap Market to open the Market app.

2. On the Incredible 2, tap Apps, and tap Books & Reference; on the Droid X2, Droid 3, and Droid Charge, tap Books.

3. Flick from right to left to Top Free.

4. Tap any book.

5. Tap Open.

6. Flick to move through the pages.

7. To access the Table of Contents, press the Menu button on your phone, and tap Contents. Tap any chapter title to go to that chapter.

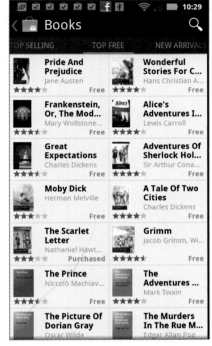

FIGURE 5-22 Purchase or obtain free books from the Market's Books section.

If you decide to purchase a book, you do so in the same manner you used to purchase an app earlier in this chapter. Tap the price button, accept and buy, and wait for the download to complete. After you obtain a few books, you can press your phone's Menu button to access your e-books; change settings such as text size, typeface, brightness, and so on; share the book with others; and more. Figure 5-23 shows these options on the Droid 3. Similar options exist on other Droid phones.

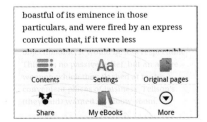

FIGURE 5-23 You can access settings related to books from the Menu button.

What may surprise you is that you don't need to tap the Market app to read the books you downloaded; you can use the Books app. On the Droid X2 and Droid 3, you can open the Books app from the Open apps screen and then tap the book you'd like to read. See Figure 5-24.

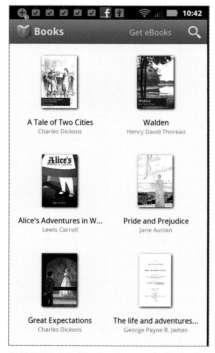

FIGURE 5-24 The Books apps is likely already on your Droid phone, and you can use it to read e-books you obtain from the Market.

SET UP CONTENT FILTERING While on any Market page (Apps, Games, Books, Movies, or the equivalent of these on the Incredible 2), press the Menu button on your phone to access Settings. Here, you can set a content filtering level. You can choose to allow apps, games, movies, and books rated for Everyone, Low Maturity, Medium Maturity, or High Maturity, or you can opt to show all the available content, no matter the content level.

About the only other thing you need to know about Books is that they're stored "in the cloud" on Google's computer servers. The nice thing about this is that those books are available from just about any device that's connected to the Internet, even PCs and Macs. Just visit `http://books.google.com/books` and log on with your Google username and password.

DOWNLOADING AND WATCHING A MOVIE

You can rent and buy movies and watch them on your Droid phone. You browse, buy, and rent movies using the same techniques you learned earlier in this chapter. You enter the Movies section by tapping Movies on the Market home screen. (On the Incredible 2, tap Apps and tap Media & Video first). When there, tap the movie to buy or rent, and tap the appropriate icon. Figure 5-25 shows an option to rent. As with other purchases, you must tap Accept & Buy (even if you're renting), before you can download the movie.

After the movie downloads, which should take only a few seconds, tap Play, as shown in Figure 5-26.

FIGURE 5-25 You can rent most movies in lieu of buying them.

FIGURE 5-26 Play becomes an option after a movie has downloaded.

HOW LONG DOES A RENTAL LAST? If you buy a movie, you own it. If you rent a movie, you have 30 days to start watching it, and then 24 hours to finish watching it once it's started.

Related Questions

+ How much data can my Droid store? **PAGE 50**
+ How do I reposition apps on the screen or organize them in folders? **PAGE 44**
+ How do I connect to a Wi-Fi network? **PAGE 101**
+ How can I find apps that can help me use my Droid better at work? **ONLINE AT www.wiley.com/go/droidcompanion**

CHAPTER SIX

HOW DO I GET THE MOST FROM MESSAGING, CHATS, AND EMAIL?

In This Chapter:

+ Sending and Receiving Text and MMS Messages
+ Using Google Talk to Chat with Others
+ Getting the Most from the Gmail App
+ Getting the Most from the Messaging and Email Apps

Texting may be the thing you do most with your Droid phone. Sure, you make calls, check email, and surf the web, but texting quickly becomes second nature. The Droid comes with an app for texting named Text Messaging, which you can use to send simple messages to others' phones. You can acquire additional messaging apps from the Market. Your Droid also comes with Talk, short for Google Talk, which is an app that enables you to hold text chats with other Google Talk users. You can also use this app to hold video chats, provided you both have compatible devices.

Another type of electronic messaging is email. If you use only a single Gmail account and no other email addresses, the Gmail app is perfect for you, and it's already set up and ready to use. If you use more than one email address, though, you need to branch out from the Gmail app. If this is the case, you can use the Messaging and Email apps. These apps enable you to easily incorporate third-party email accounts and group and view messages in various ways.

Sending and Receiving Text and Multimedia Messages

Texting and chatting (instant messaging) are two different things, and in this section you learn only about texting. You need to know the difference between texting and chatting right from the beginning to avoid confusion later.

Texting is what you do when you send a short text message to someone else's phone. You do not open a program and hope to hold an ongoing conversation; much of the time a simple text is just a few words to say, "I'm on my way" or "I love you." Because this type of universal messaging was created and is mainly used to communicate between *cell phones*, you may not send texts to devices that aren't phones, such as the Motorola Xoom or Apple's iPad, unless those users have installed a compatible texting app.

When you *chat* with someone (which is not the same as sending a text), you hold an ongoing conversation using a program both you and the recipient have open, such as Google Talk, AIM, Windows Live Messenger, and the like. You create a chat session when you need and expect some back-and-forth between you and your contact. The Droid comes with Talk for this purpose (that's Google Talk on your PC or Mac); although, you may need additional messaging programs to communicate with all your contacts (specifically those who don't use Google Talk). You can get additional chatting programs, called instant messaging programs, from the Market.

CREATING A SIMPLE TEXT MESSAGE

If you need a quick way to say, "I'm in the parking lot, where are you?" you can do it with a text. People often write a text in lieu of making a phone call because it completely eliminates the possibility of getting stuck in a long conversation on the phone! Beyond that, people often text instead of calling when they do not want to completely interrupt the person they want to communicate with. This is a great way to send a message when you know the other person is in a meeting, at the gym, in a noisy environment where the phone won't be heard, and so on.

To create a simple text message on the Droid X2 or Droid 3, follow these steps:

1. Tap the Text Messaging icon on the Home screen, as shown in Figure 6-1. If it's not there:

   A. Tap the Open Apps icon.

   B. Tap Text Messaging.

FIGURE 6-1 The Text Messaging icon looks like an envelope.

2. Tap the + sign to create a new message.

3. Begin typing the name of the contact to text or the phone number.

4. If you see the contact, as shown in Figure 6-2, tap it. If not, continue until you type the required information.

5. Tap where it says Enter Message Here, and type your message. You can type up to 160 characters.

6. If, as you type a word, you see the entire word listed under your text, you can tap that word to have your Droid complete the word for you. Of course, you can just keep typing until you enter the word.

7. Tap Send when finished.

To create a simple text message on the Droid Incredible 2 or Droid Charge, follow these steps:

1. Tap the Messages or Messaging icon on the Home screen, as shown in Figure 6-3.

2. Tap Compose Message.

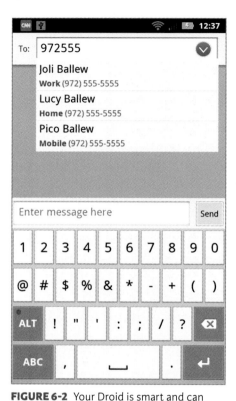

FIGURE 6-2 Your Droid is smart and can offer suggestions that match what you type.

3. Begin typing the name of the contact you want to text or the contact's phone number.

4. If you see the contact, as shown in Figure 6-4, tap it. If not, continue until you've typed the required information.

5. Tap where it says Add Text or Type to Compose, and type your message. You can type up to 160 characters.

6. If you have *only* a Droid Incredible 2, you see the entire word listed under your text as you type. You can tap that word to have your Droid complete the word for you. Of course, you can just keep on typing until you've entered the word.

7. Tap Send when finished.

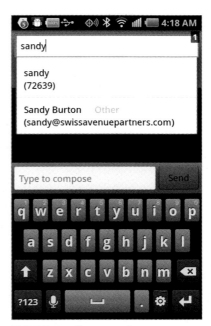

FIGURE 6-3 On some Droid phones, the Messages icon looks like a cartoon bubble.

FIGURE 6-4 If you see the contact, tap it instead of typing the entire name or number.

PUT A SHORTCUT TO THE TEXT MESSAGING APP ON THE HOME SCREEN If you think you'll often use the Text Messaging app, add it to your Home screen. Just tap the Open Apps icon, tap and hold Text Messaging, and tap Add to Home when the prompt to do so appears.

CHECKING FOR AND REPLYING TO MESSAGES

If you have your phone near you when a text arrives, you likely hear your Droid make a sound, vibrate, or do whatever it is you have configured in Sounds (under Settings). It may be that your phone says "Droid" in a low voice and vibrates, for instance. If you aren't close enough to hear or feel the text arriving, that's OK. You can see that a message has arrived on the Status bar, as shown in Figure 6-5.

CONFIGURE AND USE SWYPE Swype is a feature that's likely available on your phone, which is supposed to make it easier and faster to write texts and emails. You can access Swype settings in the Language & Keyboard screen on the Droid X2, Droid 3, and Droid Charge. Swype does not come pre-installed on the Droid Incredible 2 but you can sign up to receive the beta version of Swype from the Swype website at `www.swype.com`. After you sign up you'll receive an email message with a link to download Swype onto your Incredible 2.

Once you've accessed Swype settings you can make changes to how you enter text and what is done to it when you do. For instance, you may want to choose Espanol over English, turn on or off "word prediction," turn on or off audio feedback, turn on or off vibration feedback, enable or disable auto-capitalization, and more. There's even a Swype help user manual and a tutorial if you want to learn more.

New text message

FIGURE 6-5 The small envelope on the Status bar lets you know a new message has arrived.

To access a message that's arrived and to reply to it:

1. Hold and drag downward to view the notifications on the Status bar.
2. Tap the applicable notification. See Figure 6-6.
3. Type your message to respond, as shown in Figure 6-7.

FIGURE 6-6 The Status bar offers easy access to new text messages.

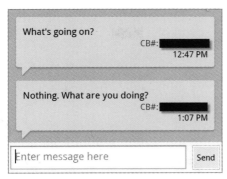

FIGURE 6-7 Type a message in the Enter Message Here area to reply to a message.

IS THERE ANY TEXTING ETIQUETTE I SHOULD BE AWARE OF?
Often, when people send you a text that is simply informative, they want to know you read it, but they don't want to be bothered with a long response. It's perfectly OK to respond to a text like "I'm on my way up to your apartment" with "K." It is often unacceptable to opt not to respond.

INSERTING EMOTICONS AND SETTING A PRIORITY

While writing a text message, you can press the Menu button on your phone to see additional options. A fun thing to add is a "smiley." These are actually called emoticons, and there are lots of them that aren't all smiley faces!

For instance, you can opt to add an emoticon that looks like a face that's winking, kissing, or yelling. You can tap More, shown with the other options in Figure 6-8, to also set a priority for the message. When an "urgent" message arrives on the recipient's phone, the message will have something beside it, often a red flag.

FIGURE 6-8 Tap the Menu button on your phone to add a little something more to your text.

To access and add emoticons and set a priority for a message on the Droid X2 or Droid 3, follow these steps:

1. Tap the Text Messaging app to open it.

2. Tap the + sign to create a new message.

3. Type a contact name or phone number in the To line.

4. Type your message.

5. Press the Menu button on your phone.

6. Tap Insert Smiley.

7. Tap the emoticon to add; you can scroll down to see more. See Figure 6-9.

8. Tap Send.

To access and add emoticons and set a priority for a message on the Droid Incredible 2 or Droid Charge, follow these steps:

FIGURE 6-9 Choose an emotion that expresses your feelings!

1. Tap the Messages or Messaging app to open it.

2. Tap Compose Message to create a new message.

3. Type a contact name or phone number in the To line.

4. Type your message.

5. Press the Menu button on your phone, and then tap More if necessary.

6. Tap Insert Smiley.

7. Tap the emoticon to add; you can scroll down to see more. Refer to Figure 6-9 for an example.

8. Tap Send.

Even though the emoticon you place inside your text message may look only like a semicolon, a few dots, and another symbol on your phone, it should appear as a graphic in your conversation list after you tap Send. When the recipients get your message, what they see depends on the phone they receive it on.

CREATING MULTIMEDIA MESSAGES

You likely saw in Figure 6-8 earlier that Insert was an option while creating a text message. If you tap Insert, you have the option to select what to insert, including an existing picture; a new picture you take with your Droid's camera; existing audio; new audio you record using your Droid's microphone; and existing video or new video you take with the Camcorder; a slideshow of pictures; your location; and a name card (contact information). When you insert media, the message is converted from a simple text message to a more complex multimedia message.

Although there's not enough room here to detail each of these options, here you learn how to record something and attach the resulting audio to an outgoing text message on the Droid X2 or Droid 3. Next, you learn how to attach a small video file on the Droid Incredible 2 and a slideshow on the Droid Charge. The process is basically the same for all phones, so it's worth reviewing each no matter what Droid phone you have.

To attach a recording of your voice or live audio to a text message on the Droid X2 and Droid 3, follow these steps:

1. Open the Text Messaging app, and address a new message.

2. Press the Menu button on your phone.

FIGURE 6-10 You can add audio to your message, among other things.

3. Tap Insert.

4. Tap New Audio. See Figure 6-10.

5. When the audio page opens, tap the circle to start recording. Talk into the microphone if you want to record your own voice.

6. Tap the square Stop button, and then tap Use This Recording. (You could tap Discard.)

7. Note the New Music icon attached to the text. Also, you can see MMS just above the Send button. Complete your message as applicable, and tap Send. See Figure 6-11.

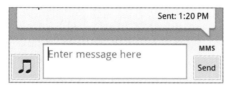

Sent: 1:20 PM

Enter message here

MMS

Send

FIGURE 6-11 When a simple text message includes media, it becomes an MMS message.

ARE THERE EXTRA COSTS AND DATA USAGE WITH MMS MESSAGES? There are indeed additional costs with multimedia messages because instead of sending simple text, which uses minimal data, you're sending media, which uses more. You should review your plan to see what costs you'll incur, if any. If you opt to pay as you go with Verizon, a simple text costs 20 cents a message, and messages with pictures and video cost a quarter. You may also have opted for a plan that enables you to send 250 messages for $5 a month, unlimited for $20, or something similar.

To attach a slideshow to a text message from a Droid Charge, follow these steps:

1. Open the Messaging app, and address a new message.

2. Press Menu.

3. Tap Attach.

4. Tap Slideshow, as shown in Figure 6-12. (You may need to scroll down to see this option.)

5. Tap the slideshow you want to edit in the Edit Slideshow screen.

6. Edit the slideshow by adding a picture and then adding text.

7. Tap Done. The slideshow appears in the Compose Message screen.

8. Type your message, and then tap Send.

To attach a small video file using a Droid Incredible 2, follow these steps:

1. Open the Messages app, and address a new message.

2. Tap the Attach icon.

3. Tap Video, as shown in Figure 6-13.

4. Tap Videos.

5. Tap All Videos in the album list.

6. Tap the video you want to add. The video appears on the Compose Message screen.

7. Type your message, and then tap Send.

FIGURE 6-12 Tap Slideshow to attach a slideshow to your message.

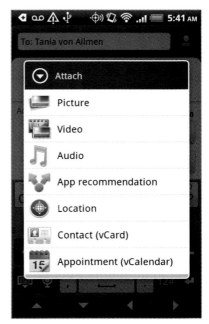

FIGURE 6-13 Tap Video to attach a video to your message.

CHECK WITH YOUR CONTACTS BEFORE SENDING TOO MANY SMS MESSAGES Because there are additional costs applied when you send an SMS (or even a text in some instances) make sure your contacts want to receive texts from you. If they're charged per text message, they may not.

RECEIVING MULTIMEDIA MESSAGES

When you receive a message that includes media, the Status bar shows a quick notification that a multimedia message has been received. When you access the message, if it's a picture, the picture automatically appears in the text message. If it's a contact card, that information appears as well. However, if it's an audio file or some other kind of media, you probably need to tap the icon that plays the sound or view the video. Figure 6-14 shows two incoming texts. The one on top is an audio file with no text; the one on the bottom is a video. You tap the icons to play the media.

FIGURE 6-14 Media appears in various forms in a text.

Using Google Talk to Chat with Others

You can use Google Talk, already on your Droid phone, to hold instant messaging conversations with others you know who also use Google Talk. You can send messages to any of those contacts who are online, or send messages that will be delivered when they come online. They, in turn, can write back, and you can hold a chat and have an "instant messaging conversation." You can even save the conversation. If you have contacts who use Google Talk, and if you both agree to be "friends" on Talk, you can see your contact in the Talk window. A green circle indicates your contact is available, as shown in Figure 6-15.

FIGURE 6-15 Green means that your contact is ready for a chat!

I DON'T SEE ANYONE LISTED WHEN I OPEN GOOGLE TALK If you don't have any Talk "friends," you need to send someone an invitation. Think of a friend who likes to chat (preferably someone who already uses Google Talk on a phone, tablet, or computer), and then, follow these steps:

1. Open Talk.
2. Press the Menu button.
3. Tap Add Friend.
4. Type the email address of the friend to invite.
5. Tap Send Invitation.
6. Wait for the person to receive the invitation and accept it. The person may also have to download and set up Google Talk.
7. Note the new friend in your Friends list in Talk.

UNDERSTANDING THE TALK WINDOW

The Talk window offers information about your contacts, mainly regarding their availability to chat with you. Following are a few things you should know about the default Talk window that shows your list of contacts:

- ✦ You can hold instant messaging conversations with all contacts who are online. A green circle indicates they are online and available. Just tap the contact, type your message, and tap Send.
- ✦ You can send a message to anyone who is not online, which will be delivered after they come online. A black icon with an X in it means a contact is offline (or invisible, meaning they are online but pretending to be offline).
- ✦ As you send messages, the order of the contacts in your Talk list changes. People you've chatted with recently are shown first.
- ✦ You can initiate a video chat with contacts who have a green Video icon by their names. Tap the contact and tap the Video icon to start. Although most Droid phones don't support this yet, they will soon.
- ✦ An orange circle with a clock in it means the contact is "away."
- ✦ A red circle means the contact is "busy."
- ✦ A blue circle means the person is idle. A user's device goes idle after a specific length of inactivity, which may be as short as a few minutes.

EXPLORE TALK SETTINGS From the Talk window that shows your contacts (press the Back button on your phone if you're in a chat), press the Menu button on your phone. Tap Settings. From there you can configure various Talk settings, including automatically signing in, setting a tone for new Talk notifications, showing a notification in the Status bar when new instant messages (IMs) arrive, and more.

CHATTING WITH GOOGLE TALK

You chat with Google Talk the same way you send and receive text messages with the Text Messaging app. You simply tap the contact, type your message, and tap Send. However, with Google Talk, you aren't charged for a text message because you aren't sending a text message! You're sending data over the Internet. The data you send is charged against your data usage allowance, though.

When in a conversation you can insert emoticons, chat "off the record" (meaning your chats can't be saved), switch to another chat session with another user, view your Friend list, clear all entries in your chat (your chat history), and add people to a chat or end a chat. You access these commands by pressing the Menu button on your phone while in a chat session. Figure 6-16 shows this. You need to tap More to access the commands you can't see.

To use Talk, follow these steps:

1. Tap the All Apps or Applications icon, and tap Talk.

2. Tap a contact to chat with who is online and available.

3. Type your message and tap Send.

4. Repeat to reply to any response.

5. To access additional options, press the Menu button on your phone.

6. Tap the wanted option. For now:

    A. Tap More.

    B. Tap Insert Smiley, as shown in Figure 6-17.

    C. Tap an emoticon to add.

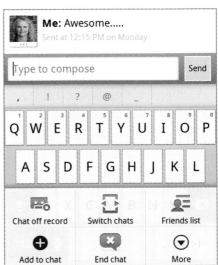

FIGURE 6-16 You can access chat options by tapping the Menu button on your phone.

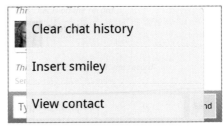

FIGURE 6-17 As with the Text Messaging app, additional options are available from the Menu button.

I DON'T KNOW ANYONE WHO USES GOOGLE TALK Your contacts may already be connected to each other through AIM, Skype, Windows Live Messenger, or other instant messaging applications, and they may not use Talk. It may be that you need to obtain a compatible third-party app to enable you to communicate with them.

To find a compatible app, go to the Market. Search for **Instant Messaging**. Read the reviews and the information offered, and download the app that looks compatible and the best for you.

HOLDING A VIDEO CHAT

With a few select Droid phones, you can send live video from your phone's video camera to another person over the Internet to hold a video chat. You do this with Google Talk. If it's possible on your phone, and you have a contact with a compatible Droid device or a contact with a PC with the required software and hardware, you see a video camera by its name. You must have a contact in Talk with a green Camera icon by the contact's name to video chat.

To have a video chat, do this:

1. On your Droid, open Talk.

2. Tap a contact that has a video camera by the contact's name.

3. Wait while your contact receives a notification you're calling and accepts the call. If your contact is at a computer and using Google Chat, it might look like what's shown in Figure 6-18.

FIGURE 6-18 When you initiate a video chat with a person at a computer, this is what the person sees.

CAN I VIDEO CHAT WHEN CONNECTED TO A 3G OR 4G NETWORK?
Yes, you certainly can, although sending and receiving video uses up quite a bit of data, so be aware of how long you visit.

Using the Gmail App

As you know, the Gmail app comes preinstalled on your Droid; often it's on the default Home screen. Additionally, because you created a Google account when you set up your Droid, you already have a Gmail (email) address, and the Gmail app is already set up for you. You'll only use the Gmail app to access your Gmail, but what you learn here you can apply to other email apps you use, so it's worth reviewing, no matter what your primary email address is.

EXPLORING THE GMAIL INTERFACE

The Gmail app enables you to easily download, read, and reply to your Gmail email. You can also preview, open, and manage compatible attachments. You can even use online tools to create your own labels (think *folders*) for Gmail and manage mail with them.

When you open Gmail, you see your "conversations," which are email messages you've received, grouped together as applicable. When you tap any email in the list (see Figure 6-19), the email opens in a new window. If an email has an attachment, you see a Paperclip icon, also shown in Figure 6-19.

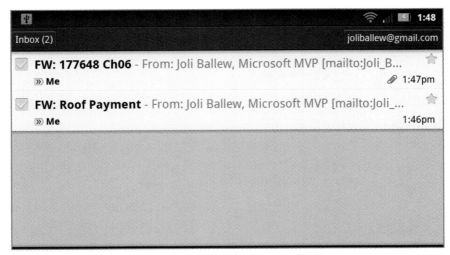

FIGURE 6-19 Unread email appears in bold in the Conversation list.

While in the view shown in Figure 6-19, you can tap the Menu button on your phone and tap Labels to see email stored in places other than your Inbox. (In the Email app, which you learn about later, Labels is replaced with Folders.) The labels you access most in the Gmail app include the following:

✤ **Inbox**—Holds email that is in your Inbox that you have not deleted or moved.

✤ **Priority Inbox**—Gmail attempts to select what email is most important to you and places copies of emails it categorizes as important here. Gmail uses a variety of signals to make this determination, including who you email with and chat with most, among other things.

✤ **Starred**—Holds email you've denoted with a star. There's a Star option on each email you open.

✤ **Chats**—Holds data related to chats you've held that Gmail thinks may be related to email you've received.

✤ **Sent**—Holds email you've previously sent.

✤ **Outbox**—Holds email you've written and sent but have not actually been sent yet. Large emails take longer to leave the Outbox than small ones, and email can't be sent if you're not connected to the Internet.

✤ **Drafts**—Holds email you've started and saved. When you're ready to complete the email, just tap the Drafts folder, tap the email, complete it, and tap Send.

✤ **All Mail**—Holds all your email, not only what has just arrived in your Inbox.

✤ **Spam**—Holds email Gmail thinks is Spam. You should check this folder occasionally for valid email. (You can mark spam by tapping the Settings icon and tapping Report spam.)

✤ **Trash**—Holds email you've deleted.

✦ **< your own labels >**—Includes any additional labels you've created. You add the labels from the Gmail website, as shown in Figure 6-20. (Note the Create New Label option.) Labels you add on the website automatically sync to your phone.

FIGURE 6-20 You can create labels easily and manage them, all from Google's Gmail website.

COMPOSING AND REPLYING TO EMAIL

When you tap any email in the view shown in Figure 6-19, the new pane that appears offers options for working with the selected email, including the option to reply to it. You can tap the left-facing arrow called out in Figure 6-21 to show additional options. When you opt to tap Reply, Reply All, or Forward, yet another view appears. This new view is simply the email, ready for you to input your response or message.

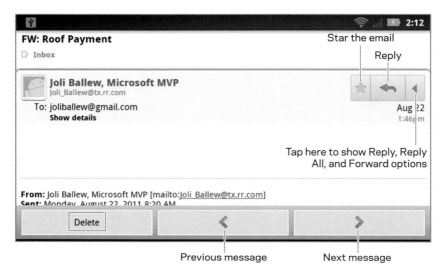

FIGURE 6-21 A lot of options are packed away in the small email window.

To compose a new email using the Gmail app, follow these steps:

1. Tap Gmail to open the app.

2. Verify you're in the Inbox. The Inbox was shown in Figure 6-19. If necessary, press the Back button on your phone to get to your Inbox. (You can also tap the Menu button and tap Go to Inbox.)

3. Tap the Menu button and tap Compose.

4. Type the email address or contact name in the To line. Tap Next.

5. Type the subject. Tap Next.

6. Type the message body, and tap Done.

7. If you'd like to save the message in the Drafts folder, tap the Save icon. It looks like an old floppy disk.

8. Press the Menu button on your phone. You can:

   A. Send the email now.

   B. Save it as a draft.

C. Add recipients in the CC or BCC lines.

D. Attach a file.

E. Discard the email.

F. Get help.

G. Press the Back button on the phone to hide the options.

9. Tap the Send icon when you're ready to send the message. See Figure 6-22.

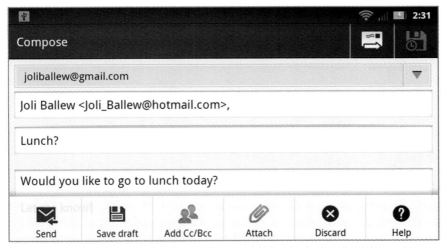

FIGURE 6-22 You'll populate familiar email areas with data including the To line, subject line, and body; you access more options by pressing the Menu button on your phone.

To reply to or forward a message you receive, follow these steps:

1. Tap Gmail to open the app.

2. Verify you're in the Inbox. The Inbox was shown in Figure 6-19. If necessary, press the Back button on your phone to get to your Inbox. (You can also tap the Menu button and tap Go to Inbox.)

3. Tap any email to respond to or forward.

4. Tap the Reply button, or tap the left-facing arrow to see Reply, Reply All, and Forward, as shown in Figure 6-23.

5. Tap the desired option and complete the email as necessary.

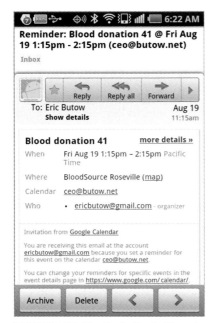

FIGURE 6-23 The Reply, Reply All, and Forward icons.

DON'T TYPE; SPEAK ON THE DROID! You are going to be blown away when you find out you don't have to type your emails anymore! When composing a message, tap in the body of the email, and then simply tap the Microphone icon. Speak what you want to type, and let your Droid do the work.

Additionally, on all Droid models you can tap the microphone icon to speak a text. You can even say something like "smiley face" and have an emoticon inserted. You'll want to experiment with this to see what's available on your phone, and how it works.

MANAGING ATTACHMENTS

Sometimes an email arrives with something attached to it. These attachments can be pictures, audio clips, short videos, documents, spreadsheets, contact cards, and more. Likewise, you can send email with your own items attached. On computers at least, attachments are often used to proliferate viruses. Although this isn't yet an issue with Droid, it's still best to only open attachments from people you know—and only attachments you expect.

Receiving and Viewing Attachments

When you receive an email with an attachment, it has a Paperclip icon on it. If the attachment is a picture, it may automatically appear in the body of the email; the same is true for other compatible files. If it's an attachment that won't automatically show itself in the body, you must tap to open it. On the Droid X2 and the Droid 3, you tap Preview, as shown in Figure 6-24. You find this option at the end of the email, so you need to scroll down.

177648 Ch06.do...
134KB

Preview

FIGURE 6-24 You can preview compatible attachments.

When you tap Preview, the attachment opens in its respective program. In this example, tapping Preview causes Quick Office to open, and the document displays in it.

On the Droid Charge and Droid Incredible 2, you tap the filename to open the document on a compatible program installed on your device. For example, you can open a Microsoft Word file in Quick Office.

WHAT HAPPENS WHEN MULTIPLE APPS CAN OPEN THE SAME FILE TYPE? If you have two apps that can open the same file type, when you tap Preview in Gmail, you'll be prompted to choose which app to use.

To open an email view or preview its attachment, follow these steps on the Droid X2 or Droid 3:

1. If necessary, send yourself an email with an attachment from your desktop computer.

2. In Gmail, access your Inbox.

3. Press the Menu button, and tap Refresh to have Gmail check for new mail.

4. Tap the email that contains the attachment.

5. Scroll down to the bottom of the email, and tap Preview.

6. If it's a large attachment, it may take some time to open.

To open an email view or preview its attachment, follow these steps on the Droid Incredible 2 or Droid Charge:

1. If necessary, send yourself an email with an attachment from your desktop computer.

2. In Gmail, access your Inbox.

3. Press the Menu button, and tap Refresh to have Gmail check for new mail.

4. Tap the email that contains the attachment.

5. Tap the attachment filename. If you have more than one app installed that can open the attachment, select the app to use.

6. If it's a large attachment, it may take some time to open.

Saving an Attachment

If you want to save an attachment, you have three options. You can move the email to a folder you've previously created at your Gmail web page. You can download the attachment to your internal storage card. You can preview the attachment in a program such as Quick Office and access the Save or Save As command from there. (The same holds true later when you use the Email app.)

The easiest, in Gmail at least, is to save the email that contains the attachment by assigning it a label. This copies the email and its attachment to that folder where you can access it later. Then, you can remove the email from your Inbox by tapping Archive. (Don't delete the email or it will be removed, even from your labels!) Before you start, visit www.google.com/gmail from your computer, and create a few labels. Consider Notes, School, or Travel, for starters.

To assign a label to an email message and to remove the message from your Inbox, follow these steps:

1. Open the email message to save.

2. Press Menu.

3. Tap Change Labels.

4. Tap the label name.

5. Tap OK. See Figure 6-25.

6. Back at the email, tap Archive if necessary. A green bar appears at the top of the email list informing you that the message has been archived.

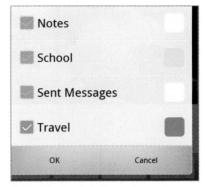

If you don't want to keep the email, you can download the attachment. Download is an option when a picture arrives in an email, among other things. When you download something, it's stored on your phone's internal storage or SD card. You can find the down-loaded item in the appropriate app. For instance, if you opt to download a picture in Gmail, you can find it later in the Gallery app under My Library. Figure 6-26 shows the Download but-ton on a Droid 3. After you download the attachment, you can delete the email. (In the Email app, detailed later, you tap the icon that looks like a floppy disk to save an attachment.)

Finally, you may preview the attach-ment and save it using whatever program you used to open it. The directions for doing this differ from app to app, but often pressing the Menu button offers options you use most. When saved, you can then delete the email.

FIGURE 6-25 Labels are the easiest way to save an attachment you want to access later.

FIGURE 6-26 When you download a pic-ture, it's saved automatically to the Gallery.

Attaching Items to an Outgoing Email

You can attach your own files to email you create in Gmail, provided you can find them. To add an attachment to an email in Gmail, follow these steps:

1. In Gmail, press the Menu button on the phone, and tap Compose.

2. Fill in the To line, the Subject line, and add your message.

3. Press Menu and then tap Attach. (In the Email app, detailed later, the command is Attach Files.)

4. Tap Files to locate a file, or tap Gallery to locate a picture.

5. Tap Internal Phone Storage, SD Card, or Shared Folders, as applicable.

6. Find and tap the item to attach.

7. Note the attachment, as shown in Figure 6-27.

8. Complete the email as wanted, and tap Send.

FIGURE 6-27 You'll know the attachment was successful if you see a paperclip icon on your new email message.

Although there's more to Gmail than covered here, this is a good start, and many of the things you can do with the Gmail app you can also do in the Email app. (So there is some overlap of functionality if you keep reading.)

Before leaving this section, though, explore the Settings options. While in the Gmail Inbox, press the Menu button on your phone, and tap Email Settings to see more options. You can configure options for email delivery, composing, displaying, and even creating out-of-office replies. And although you can't choose a font while you write an email in Gmail, you do have the option to choose a different font than the one used now. Figure 6-28 shows these options, and as you can see, you can choose a new font, choose a font size, choose a font color, and more.

FIGURE 6-28 There's more to explore in Gmail; check out Email Settings ⇨ Compose Options for starters.

INCORPORATING THIRD-PARTY ACCOUNTS WITH GMAIL If you want to combine other email accounts with your Gmail account, and thus receive that email from the Gmail app, you should visit `http://mail.google` `.com` to review your options. You can import mail and contacts from other accounts, send mail from another address, add a POP3 account, and more. It's rather complicated, though, so before you attempt it, ensure the Messaging app and the Email app, along with associated widgets, won't better suit your needs.

Using the Messaging and Email Apps

You can configure additional third-party email accounts from the Settings page on your Droid and then access them from the Messaging app. Third-party email accounts can open in the Mail or Email app. The Email app offers functionality not available in the Gmail app, including the capability to format text in the body of an email, access other accounts quickly, and more. And although the Email app's interface looks a little different than what you saw earlier in Gmail, it's not so different that you can't infer what can happen when you tap an icon or press the Menu button on your phone.

SETTING UP ADDITIONAL EMAIL ACCOUNTS

You must tell your Droid about your third-party email accounts, including the actual email addresses and associated passwords. Depending on the account you add, you may also need to input other information that you must get from your ISP, such as incoming and outgoing mail server names, security settings, or port numbers. It's difficult to detail what you must do, though; it's best to show you how to let your Droid try to automatically configure your email, and if that doesn't work, show you how to manually input the information.

From the Droid X2 and the Droid 3, to configure new accounts, follow these steps:

1. From any Home screen, press the Menu button on your phone.
2. Tap Settings; then tap Accounts.

3. Tap Add Account.

4. Tap Email.

5. Type your email address and password, as shown in Figure 6-29.

6. Make sure that Automatically Configure Accounts is selected, and tap Next. (Next is under the virtual keyboard; it is not shown here).

7. If your account can be automatically set up, you're finished; only you need to tap OK and Done to complete the setup.

8. If the account can't be set up, tap Set Up Manually. Then:

   A. From the configuration screen tap General Settings, and appropriately configure the settings. Tap OK.

   B. Tap Incoming Server; type the incoming server name you obtained from your ISP. Verify your username and password, if your ISP requires it. Tap Advanced Settings if

FIGURE 6-29 Configure your email accounts before using the Email app.

you need to insert a port number or configure other security settings. Tap OK. (Tap OK again if necessary.)

   C. Tap Outgoing Server; type the outgoing server name you obtained from your ISP. Verify your username and password, if your ISP requires it. Tap Advanced Settings if you need to insert a port number or configure other security settings. Tap OK. (Tap OK again if necessary.)

9. Tap OK, read what's shown in Figure 6-30, and tap Done. What you see may differ.

On the Droid Charge or the Droid Incredible 2, to add email accounts, follow these steps:

1. Open the Apps (or Applications) screen, and then tap Mail or Email. (You may need to scroll through the apps list to find it.)

2. Tap Others or Other (POP3/IMAP).

3. Type your account email address and password in the boxes, and then tap Next.

4. Select the protocol for the account.

5. Set or type the following incoming server settings, as shown in Figure 6-31, as necessary:

   A. Username

   B. Password

   C. Server name

   D. Server port

   E. Security type

6. If you have *only* the Droid Incredible 2, tap Next.

7. Set or type the following outgoing server settings as necessary:

   A. Server name

   B. Server port

   C. Security type

   D. Require login or sign-in

   E. Use Verizon email gateway

8. If you have *only* the Droid Charge, select the email check frequency from the list, and then tap Next.

FIGURE 6-30 Hopefully, you see a Success! screen after inputting your email information.

9. Type your account name and your name, and then tap Done or Finish Setup.

10. The Mail or Email app fetches email from your inbox and displays it on the screen, as shown in Figure 6-32.

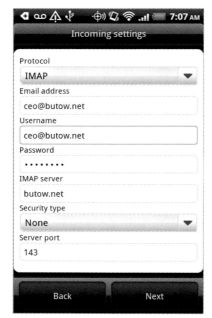

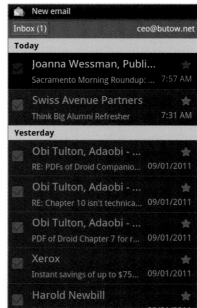

FIGURE 6-31 Set or type the incoming server settings in the Incoming Settings screen on the Droid Incredible 2.

FIGURE 6-32 The list of messages in your Inbox folder appears after you finish setting up your email account.

If you don't see the Success screen or if you find your email isn't configured properly, you need to troubleshoot it. To access the account to edit it on the Droid X2 or Droid 3, follow these steps:

1. Tap the Open Apps icon.

2. Tap Accounts.

3. Tap and hold the Account to edit.

4. Tap Open Account.

5. Edit as necessary.

To access the account settings for editing on the Droid Charge, follow these steps:

1. Open the Mail or Email app as you did earlier, and open your Inbox folder.
2. Press Menu and then tap Accounts.
3. Tap and hold your finder on the account name, and then tap Account Settings.
4. Scroll down the list and then verify your incoming and outgoing server settings.

To access the account settings for editing on the Droid Incredible 2, follow these steps:

1. Open the Mail or Email app as you did earlier, and open your Inbox folder.
2. Press Menu, and then tap More.
3. Tap Settings, and then tap Account Settings.
4. Check your incoming and outgoing server settings by following the prompts on the screen.

ACCESSING EMAIL ACCOUNTS

You can access your configured email accounts in various ways. For instance, you can open the Email app, configure a default email address from the Email Settings page, and use that app as your main email program. If you have a Droid X2 or Droid 3, a better option is to use the Messaging app.

- -

ADD THE MESSAGING APP TO THE HOME SCREEN The Messaging app is cool. With it you can get a quick glance of how many new, unread emails have arrived. You can get emails from a specific account. You can even view all your messages in a single place, the Universal Inbox. You can also view messages from Twitter, Facebook, and other entities. To add the Messaging app to the Home screen, follow these steps:

1. Tap the Open Apps icon.
2. Tap and hold Messaging.
3. Tap Add to Home.

- -

To start on the Droid X2 or the Droid 3, follow these steps:

1. Tap the Open Apps icon.

2. Tap Messaging. The Messaging app is shown in Figure 6-33.

3. To see all messages, tap Universal Inbox.

4. To see only text messages, tap Text Messaging.

5. To access a specific email account, tap its icon.

FIGURE 6-33 The Messaging app offers access to all your configured accounts.

WORKING WITH THIRD-PARTY EMAIL

Hopefully, you can draw from what you already know about the Gmail app and what you already know about emailing in general to figure out how to use the

Email app without a lot more instruction. Like the Gmail app detailed earlier, you can reply to and forward email, and you can easily delete email. (Tap the Trash icon.) From the Inbox, you can also access settings to select all email in the list, compose and email, refresh the view, and more. Although there's not enough room here to discuss all that you can do, following is a short exercise to work through to become familiar with the Email interface.

On the Droid X2 and the Droid 3, to become familiar with the Email interface, follow these steps:

1. Tap Messaging.

2. Tap a third-party email account, preferably one from your personal ISP such as Time Warner.

3. In the Inbox, flick up and down to view the emails in the list. See Figure 6-34.

4. Press the Menu button on your phone to see the options. Tap Email settings.

5. Review your email options, including but not limited to:

   A. **Notifications**—To change what happens when you receive an email

   B. **Read Options**—To change the text size for reading email

   C. **Out of Office**—To create an out-of-office reply

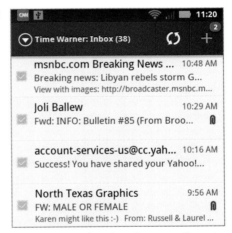

FIGURE 6-34 The Inbox shows emails you've received; tap once to open.

6. Press the Back button on your phone; then tap any email to open it.

7. Tap the Reply button. See the options Reply, Reply All, and Forward.

8. Press the Back button on your phone.

9. Tap the up and down arrows to move to other messages in your Inbox.

10. Tap the Trash icon to delete an email.

On the Droid Charge and the Incredible 2, follow these steps:

1. Tap Mail or Email on the Home screen.

2. If necessary, select a third-party email account.

3. In the Inbox, flick up and down to view the emails in the list, as shown in Figure 6-35.

4. Press the Menu button, and then tap More to get other options. Tap Settings or Account Settings.

5. Review your email options, including but not limited to:

   A. Notification settings to change what happens when you read an email message

   B. Signature settings to change what appears automatically at the end of your message when you send it

   C. The mail size limit to determine the size of messages that you are willing to receive on your Droid

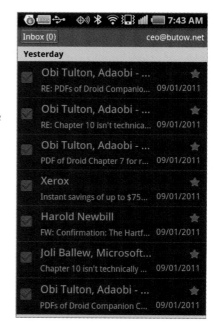

FIGURE 6-35 The Inbox shows emails you've received; flick up and down to review then, and tap on the email once to open.

6. Press Back (twice if you have the Incredible 2) and then type any message to open it.

7. Tap the Reply button. See the options below the text box.

8. Press Back and discard your message. You may need to press Back once or twice more to return to the Inbox.

9. Flick up and down to move to other messages in your Inbox.

10. Delete a message by tapping the check box to the left of the sender name and then tapping Delete.

USE A MESSAGES WIDGET If you can find a Messages widget, add it. On the Motorola Droid X2, the widget is listed under Motorola widgets. Widgets are interactive. In the case of the Motorola widget, you can flick left and right to move among messages. You can also easily reply or delete a message. With this widget you can compose and write an email using the Email app.

Related Questions

+ How can I incorporate social networking? **PAGE 240**
+ Where can I get instant messaging apps and email widgets? **PAGE 120**
+ How can I manage my networking features such as Wi-Fi and cellular? **PAGE 100**
+ How can I incorporate contacts with email? **PAGE 80**

CHAPTER SEVEN

HOW DO I GET THE MOST FROM THE WEB?

In This Chapter:

+ Customizing Browser Settings
+ Navigating with the Browser
+ Using Flash
+ Downloading Files
+ Exploring Other Browsers

Another great feature of the Droid family is the ability to access the web so that you can connect with others, find information, and even show web-based information to others—all in the palm of your hand. All four Droid phones come with the Browser app built in.

The Browser icon is on the default Home screen. On the Droid Incredible 2, the browser icon is called Internet. On the Droid Charge, the icon is called Browser. On both these phones, the icon for the Browser is a globe. On the Droid X2 and the Droid 3, it looks more like a flat globe—although it's still a map of the world! No matter which flavor of Droid you use, the Browser shown in Figure 7-1 takes you to the Internet.

FIGURE 7-1 The Browser globe icon is on the Droid Charge.

Customizing Browser Settings

Before you start surfing, you need to customize the Browser settings so that you get everything you want and keep out what you don't.

VIEW IN HORIZONTAL OR VERTICAL

If screen auto-rotation is on (and it is by default on all Droid models), you can rotate the screen 90 degrees to see the Browser in horizontal mode, as shown in Figure 7-2. This view is useful if you like longer lines of text and like to view images online. It's also easier to search in horizontal mode because the search box is larger and so is the keyboard, as you see in the next section.

You can search the web by tapping the Search icon, which is the soft or hard button at the right of the button bar below the screen. When you open search, the Search window appears and displays the Search screen shown in Figure 7-3.

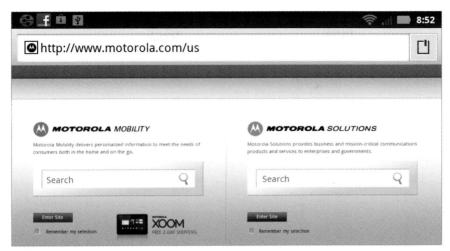

FIGURE 7-2 The Browser is in horizontal mode on the Droid X2.

FIGURE 7-3 This is the search screen on the Droid Incredible 2.

SEARCH BY VOICE IN THE BROWSER The Droid Incredible 2 has a nifty search feature that appears between the hide keyboard button and the comma button at the lower-left end of the keyboard (to the left of the spacebar). It looks like a microphone, and when you tap it you can speak your search term into the phone and then tap OK. Note that you must speak slowly and enunciate clearly so you give the Droid the best chance of finding what you're looking for. If you don't, the Browser may return some strange interpretation of your search term(s).

After you've spoken your search term, the Droid Incredible 2 searches the web for what you've spoken when you're in the Browser app.

The Droid Charge enables you to search by voice but not directly from the Browser. You have to open the Applications screen, scroll to page 3, and then tap Voice Search. After you finish speaking, the Droid Charge searches the web and other search locations that you specify in Settings. Alternatively, you can add the Google Search widget to the Home screen for faster access.

The Droid X2 and the Droid 3 both offer a Voice Search icon inside the Browser. The best way to get to it is to press the hard or soft Search button on your phone while using the Browser.

For every phone, you can add the option to search the web with your voice by adding the Google Search widget to any Home screen.

CHANGING THE SEARCH PROVIDER

All Droid models enable you to search using Google by default. If you want to change the search engine, you have slim pickings. You can choose from one of the three major search engines: Google, Yahoo!, and Bing. If you prefer one of the other two engines to Google, or you want to change back to Google after a while, here's how to do it:

1. Tap Browser on the Home screen if you're not in the Browser already.
2. Press the Menu button below the screen.

3. Tap More.

4. Tap Settings.

5. Scroll down (almost to the end of the list) and tap Set Search Engine. Tap one of the search engines in the list shown in Figure 7-4.

CHANGING THE HOME PAGE

Your Droid's Browser opens to a specific home page, but you probably want to personalize the web experience on your Droid by setting your own home page to open when you fire up the Browser app. Follow these steps to change your home page in any Droid device:

1. Tap the Browser or Internet icon.

2. Browse to the page to use as your home page.

3. Press the Menu button below the screen.

4. Tap More.

5. Tap Settings.

6. Tap Set Home Page.

7. Tap Use Current or Use Current Page depending on the Droid model you're using. See Figure 7-5.

8. Tap OK. The new home page appears in the Settings screen.

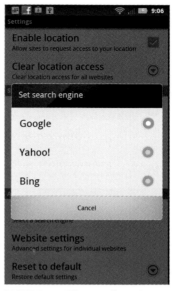

FIGURE 7-4 The search engine list appears in the Droid 3 browser.

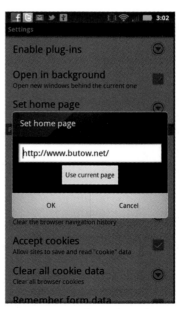

FIGURE 7-5 Configure the web page you visit most as your Home page.

CHANGING SECURITY SETTINGS

For web security, you can never be too careful. Plenty of people are eager to exploit your Droid phone for information through the web. All four Droid models address web security issues and more, so you can have a safe and secure web experience time after time.

To access these options on any Droid phone, follow these steps:

1. Tap the Browser or Internet icon on the Home screen.

2. Press the Menu button.

3. Tap More.

4. Tap Settings. (Leave this open to access more options outlined in future sections.)

Enable JavaScript

JavaScript is a language implemented on many websites that enhances the functionality of websites. For example, many websites use popup boxes that are produced by JavaScript code. All JavaScript code isn't run on the server running the website, though—it's run by the browser that's visiting the website. That means the website with JavaScript runs more quickly, but it also means that in some cases a malicious person may decide to exploit that code to get data through your browser.

With today's modern browsers, including the Browser app on the Droid phones, security issues have been mostly eliminated. However, you may decide that you want to be completely safe and disable JavaScript so it doesn't run on any of your sites. If you disable JavaScript, be aware that you won't see any JavaScript functionality on any site you visit. For example, if a website requires you to fill out a form written in JavaScript, you won't see the form on the website—you'll just see a blank space.

If you still want to disable JavaScript, scroll down until you see Enable JavaScript, as shown in Figure 7-6. The box is checked by default.

Tap Enable Plug-Ins. Note the options for enabling or disabling Browser plug-ins in the list shown in Figure 7-7. Plug-ins are programs that extend the functionality of the Browser app.

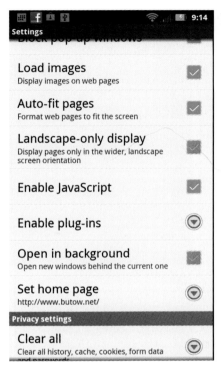

FIGURE 7-6 The Enable JavaScript check box appears on a Droid 3.

FIGURE 7-7 The Enable plug-ins option on a Droid X2.

Accept or Delete Cookie and Form Data

By default, any information you enter into online forms is saved in the Browser app. This information, called a "cookie," is stored in a database of cookies on your Droid so websites you visit can keep track of your browsing habits. Any Droid device makes it easy for you to turn these features on and off, as shown in Figure 7-8.

1. Scroll down until you see Accept Cookies. The check box is checked by default, which means websites can save and read cookies. Turn this function off by tapping the check box to clear it.

2. Tap Clear All Cookie Data and then tap OK to remove cookies from your system.

3. By default the Remember Form Data check box is checked, which means data you type in website forms will be remembered for later use. If you don't want the Browser to remember your form data for use later, tap Remember Form Data to clear the check box.

4. You can clear all saved form data by tapping Clear Form Data and then tapping Yes. (Tap OK on the Droid X2 and Droid 3.)

Location and Password Settings

Some websites ask for access to your location, so the sites can provide more detailed information for your area. For example, if you're on the road, a website that knows where you are can provide information about hotels, restaurants, and other amenities. By default, the Enable Location check box is checked so websites can see where you are. If you want to disable this function, tap Enable Location to clear the check box as shown in Figure 7-9. If you want to clear location information for all websites that you already visited, tap Clear Location Access, and then tap Yes or OK, as applicable.

By default, your Droid remembers usernames and passwords for each site you visited previously, so the next time you log in, you don't need to think about

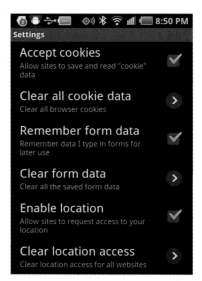

FIGURE 7-8 Use options to accept or delete cookie and form data on the Droid.

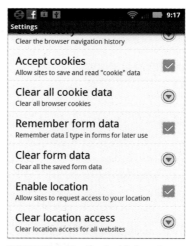

FIGURE 7-9 Use the Enable Location and Clear Location Access setup options.

what the username and password are for the site. However, this can be a security concern if you lose your phone and you don't want others to gain access to your sites.

As also shown in Figure 7-9, you can tell the Droid not to save usernames by tapping Remember Passwords. You can also clear all saved passwords from websites you've visited previously by tapping Clear Passwords and then tapping Yes or OK.

Advanced Settings and Alerts

If the Browser finds a problem with a site's security, the Browser displays a security warning in case you don't want to continue to browse the site. The Show Security Warnings check box is checked by default so you receive these warnings. If you would rather not receive them, tap Show Security Warnings to clear the check box, as shown in Figure 7-10.

NO WARNINGS DOESN'T EQUAL SAFETY Hiding the security warnings doesn't mean the site is secure. It only means you can browse unsecured sites without the Browser alerting you to the potential danger.

Individual Website Settings

Some websites you visit may transfer specific settings to your Browser so the websites can run correctly. Google has done this by default with one or more of its websites depending on what Droid model you're using. For example, the Droid Incredible 2 has advanced website settings for Google's main site (google.com) and Google's United Kingdom main site (google.co.uk). Within each site are specific settings that you can manipulate, such as removing stored data that Google's main site places on your phone to make the site run faster.

If you would rather reset all your Browser settings to their defaults, tap Reset to default, and then tap Yes or OK.

FIGURE 7-10 The Show Security Warnings setting gives you the option to turn website security warnings on or off.

To view advanced settings for websites you've visited and those you've bookmarked, tap Website Settings. Figure 7-11 shows a list of websites on the screen.

When you tap the website name, a list of setting information and options appears on the screen. For example, if the site can currently access your location via the web, you can tap Clear Location Access to block access to your location.

FIGURE 7-11 You can modify advanced settings for individual websites such as disabling location access so Google can't find your Droid when you're online.

Navigating with the Browser

Though web browsers have become much easier to use in the past few years (especially after Internet Explorer got some much-needed competition), the small form factor of any smartphone makes it more difficult to navigate through websites. Although the Droids can't match the functionality afforded by larger screen real estate, the Browser on the Droid models does a good job of fitting in a lot of functionality within a small space.

To navigate in the Browser, follow these steps:

1. Enter the website address by tapping the Address box, typing the name, and then tapping the green Enter key or the Go key. In Figure 7-12 the Browser suggests sites for you to visit under the Address box.

FIGURE 7-12 A list of suggested websites to visit appears under the Address box.

2. Refresh the page by tapping the following:

   A. The Refresh button to the right of the Address box on the Incredible.

   B. The Menu button and then Refresh on the Droid Charge.

   C. The Menu button and Refresh on the Droid X2 or Droid 3.

3. To move back and forward to pages you've already viewed, do the following:

   A. On the Droid Incredible 2 press the Menu button and then tap Back and Forward to move one page backward and one page forward, respectively. If there are no further pages in the cache before or after the last page, the Back or Forward button is unavailable.

   B. On the Droid Charge, press the Back button to move back one page. Move forward one page by pressing the Menu button and then tapping Forward. If there are no further pages in the cache after the last page, the Forward button is unavailable.

   C. On the Droid X2 and Droid 3, use the Back button on the phone to move back a page, and press the Menu button and tap Forward to move ahead.

4. To view website options, press the Menu button and tap More. Figure 7-13 shows the options on the Droid 3. From there you can do the following:

   A. Tap Find on Page to find specific text on the page you are currently viewing.

   B. Tap Select Text to select text on the page you are currently viewing. Note the different options for copying and sharing text and looking up the text definition online.

   C. Tap Share Page to share the web page with others. Check out the different options for sharing the page.

   D. Note the other options available in the list.

Add bookmark
Menu+a

Find on page
Menu+f

Save page
Menu+v

Select text
Menu+e

Page info
Menu+g

FIGURE 7-13 A list of options appear for accessing information about the website and sharing the website with others.

OPENING MULTIPLE WEB PAGES

Recent versions of web browsers on desktops and laptops added the ability to view different websites in tabs within the same browser window. This was a dramatic improvement over the old way of opening a new browser for every website and switching between browser windows. The Droid Browser also enables you open and navigate between windows when you press the Menu button on your phone.

To open and navigate between Browser windows in the Droid X2, Droid 3, and Droid Incredible 2, follow these steps:

1. Press the Menu button.

2. Tap Windows.

3. Tap the + icon above and to the left of the open window, as shown in Figure 7-14, or tap New Window below the current web page, as applicable.

4. The new window appears on the page. On the Droid X2 and Droid 3, the home screen you previously configured opens.

5. Press the Menu button and then tap Windows again.

6. On the Droid Charge, flick the web page windows left and right to switch between window views. On the Droid X2 and Droid 3, select the page to navigate to.

7. Tap and scroll through the web page to open it in full screen mode.

8. The Droid Charge makes opening a new window even easier. Press the Menu button and then tap New Window. After you tap New Window, your default home page appears in a full screen Browser window.

FIGURE 7-14 Use the Add New Window button above and to the left of the open window.

DELVING INTO SITE HISTORY

If you want to see the sites you've visited so that you can go back to a specific web page, the Browser makes it easy to see the sites you visited during the current day and up to 7 days in the past. Following are the steps to view your site history in the Droid Incredible 2:

1. Press the Menu button.
2. Tap More.
3. Tap History.
4. The list of web pages you've visited appear. The web pages are categorized by date, and you can open a web page in your history list by tapping on it.

Following is a different method to view your site history in the Droid Charge:

1. Tap the Bookmarks icon, as shown in Figure 7-15.
2. Tap History.
3. The list of web pages you've visited appears. The web pages are categorized by date, and you can open a web page in your history list by tapping it.

FIGURE 7-15 The Bookmarks icon appears to the right of the Address box.

On the Droid X2 and the Droid 3, follow these steps:

1. While in the Browser, press the Menu button.
2. Tap Bookmarks.
3. Tap History.
4. Tap the day to revisit.
5. Tap any page to navigate to it.

CREATING AND MANAGING BOOKMARKS

Like any browser, the Droid Browser enables you to bookmark websites. Bookmarks enable you to visit a website without needing to type in the website address each time. Just open the list of bookmarks, tap the bookmark to open the associated website, and there you are.

Droid Incredible 2 and Droid 3

Follow these steps to create and manage your bookmarks on the Droid Incredible 2 and Droid 3:

1. Press the Menu button.

2. To access the Add bookmark screen:

   A. On the Droid Incredible 2, tap Add bookmark.

   B. On the Droid 3, tap More and then tap Add Bookmark.

3. Type the bookmark name in the Name field, or accept what's there, and then tap Done or OK. The bookmark appears as a thumbnail image in the Bookmarks page.

4. Press the Menu button.

5. Tap Bookmarks. A tiled list of bookmarked websites appears, as shown in Figure 7-16.

6. Hold down your finger on the bookmark to open the bookmark options menu. Note the choices available to you.

7. Press the Back button.

8. Press the Menu button. Note the choices available.

FIGURE 7-16 The Bookmarks tiled list appears.

Droid X2

On the Droid X2, follow these steps to create and manage bookmarks:

1. Navigate to the page you want to bookmark.

2. Press the Menu button and tap Bookmarks.

3. The current page appears in the foreground. Tap Add.

4. Tap OK.

5. Press the Back button to return to the Browser.

6. To see and access your bookmarks:

   A. Press the Menu button.

   B. Tap Bookmarks.

   C. From the Bookmarks tab, flick to locate the desired bookmark.

   D. Tap it to access the page.

Droid Charge

Here's how to create bookmarks on the Droid Charge:

1. Navigate to the page you want to bookmark.

2. Tap the Bookmark icon.

3. Tap Add.

4. In the Add Bookmark screen, type the name of the bookmark and then tap OK.

5. Your new bookmark appears in the Bookmarks page. Press the Back button to return to the Browser.

Using Flash

There has been a lot of controversy about Apple's decision to exclude Adobe Flash from its line of smartphones and tablets for displaying multimedia content on web pages. Apple decided to go with the HTML 5 standard instead. The Android operating system and by extension the Droid family don't have that problem because Google fully supports both Flash and HTML 5.

All four models of the Droid covered in this book are preloaded with either Adobe Flash Player 10.1 or 10.2, but Adobe is always publishing updates as time goes on. As of this writing, version 10.3 is available from the Android Market, which is accessible from your home page. Even better, the

Flash Player is free. All you need to do is search for the Flash Player (it's in the Apps ⇨ Tools section shown in Figure 7-17 and download it. After you install it, you can view Flash content on any website that includes it.

FIGURE 7-17 The Flash Player application appears in the Android Market.

CHECK FLASH WHEN YOU UPGRADE ANDROID Although Flash supported all versions of Android supported by all four Droid phones covered in this book, Adobe continues to improve it, and at some point in the future, the Flash Player may require a newer version of Android. Be sure that you update your phone with the latest system updates before you upgrade your version of the Flash Player.

Downloading Files

There is practically no limit to the types of files you can download from websites, though that doesn't necessarily mean you should...or can. Types of files you can download include:

✚ Images displayed on a website. You can download any image by holding your finger down on the image until the Save Image menu appears as shown in Figure 7-18. Then tap Save Image to save it to your microSD card.

✚ Text displayed on a website by selecting the text, copying the text to the clipboard, and then pasting it to another app such as an email message.

✚ Android Market apps, which you learned about in Chapter 5. The Market is the only location for supported Android apps, which means that it not only has the official blessing of Google but also of the various cell phone companies that sell Android smartphones.

✚ Apps from the web. Type **android download sites** in Google and you'll see there is no shortage of Android apps outside of the Market. However, the cell phone company that sold you your phone may not allow you to install and/or run any app they don't approve of.

FIGURE 7-18 Tap Save Image in the Save Image menu to save the selected image on a website to your microSD card.

You download files from websites on the Droid as you do on any other device that can access the web. After you finish downloading the file, you can open the downloaded file in your download history to open the file, extract the files contained within if required, and then either open the file or install the program.

SO EVERYTHING ON THE WEB IS FREE AND SAFE, RIGHT? Not at all, so get that thought out of your head right now.

If you aren't careful when you download some files (like movies) you may run afoul of the law. If you don't know where a file comes from, you can run the risk of having your Droid's security compromised or even rendered unusable. Even text on a website may well be copyrighted so you can't just lift someone's work off a website without that someone's express permission. In sum, err on the side of caution when it comes to downloading web-based materials.

To open the Download history page in all four Droid models covered in this book, follow these steps:

1. Tap the Browser or Internet icon if you haven't opened the Browser app already.

2. Press the Menu button.

3. Tap More.

4. Tap Downloads. (You may have to scroll down.) The Downloads screen appears, as shown in Figure 7-19.

5. Tap a downloaded file in the list to open the file or run the program.

6. Press the Menu button and note the options available.

FIGURE 7-19 The Downloads page appears.

Exploring Other Browsers

The pre-installed Browser is not your only option for surfing the web. If you search for **web browsers** in the Android Market, you'll see a list of available browsers, shown in Figure 7-20, from ones that you have probably heard of, such as Firefox and Opera, and others you may not have heard of or seen before.

You might want to switch browsers for several reasons:

As you can see in Figure 7-21, the Opera Mini Browser is quite intuitive, offers Back and Forward buttons on the screen, and enables you to refresh the page without pressing the Menu button.

Dolphin HD, which is another popular alternative browser for the Android platform, has a sidebar you can access from the browser. You can also put links to sites in Speed Dial, which lets you access the sites you visit most often quickly instead of having to poke through your bookmarks.

Skyfire is another popular alternate browser for one big reason: It will play many Flash videos that may not be able to

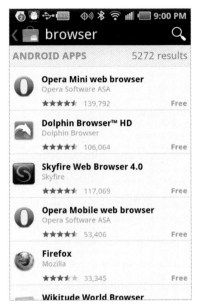

FIGURE 7-20 The first page of the list of web browsers in the Android Market.

FIGURE 7-21 Third-party browsers offer features you won't find in the Android Browser app.

play on the pre-installed Browser or on mobile devices altogether. If Skyfire finds the video won't play in Flash format, Skyfire converts the Flash to HTML 5 on its servers and feeds you the converted video. The only bad news is that this muscled-up video capability isn't free—you get a free 3-day trial and then you have to pay $2.99 for it. These and other browsers offer additional perks, including:

✛ Tabbed browsing just as you have on your desktop.

✛ Auto-completion functions where the browser will automatically complete web addresses in the Address bar.

✛ You can customize the look and feel of your browser through the use of plug-ins that you download separately.

✛ Integration with social networking sites such as Facebook and Twitter.

Android browsers are better and more competitive than ever before, and so it is worth your time and effort to explore these other browsers. You can download a new browser from the Android Market and install it as you learned in Chapter 5.

WHAT IF I DON'T SEE MY BROWSER? If you're an Internet Explorer fan, you're out of luck—Microsoft obviously won't create a browser for a competing mobile operating system. What's more surprising is that Google doesn't produce its Chrome browser for Android. Apparently there are some internal and external reasons for that, but that doesn't mean there is a dearth of available browsers out there. You might discover a new browser to fall in love with.

Related Questions

✛ How can I connect to the Internet and surf freely, without incurring any data charges? **PAGE 100**

✛ Where can I get new browsers and other apps? **PAGE 120**

✛ Where can I find the Google Search widget and add it to my Home screens? **PAGE 37**

✛ How can I use social media and the web effectively? **PAGE 196**

CHAPTER EIGHT

HOW DO I GET THE MOST FROM SOCIAL MEDIA INTEGRATION?

In This Chapter:

+ Integrating with Facebook
+ Integrating with Twitter
+ Using Friend Stream for HTC Droid Incredible 2

Integrating with Facebook

On my desktop browser I have three tabs open at all times. One of them is Facebook. I find the interface easy to use, and it's easy for me not only to update my Facebook friends about what's happening with me but also to update people about my business. I can catch up with friends and acquaintances, especially people I didn't know well in high school. (Hey, look! A former cheerleader-now-elementary-school-teacher just commented about a picture I posted on my profile.)

I'm one of millions of people—and you, too, most likely—who consider Facebook their "social stock ticker" and an invaluable part of their lives. So it's no surprise that Facebook has produced a free app for Android so that you can give and get updates while you're on the go.

DOWNLOADING THE FACEBOOK ANDROID APP

The first step is to download the Facebook app from the Android Market. After you download the app, Droid installs the app automatically.

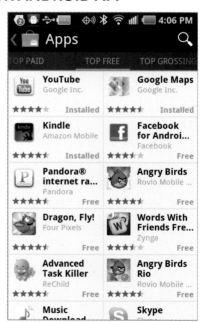

Follow these steps to download the app to your Droid:

1. Tap Market.

2. Navigate to the Market's Home screen, if applicable, and tap Apps.

3. At the top of the Apps page, flick left to the Top Free page, as shown in Figure 8-1. In the Droid Incredible 2, scroll down, tap Social, and then tap Top Free.

FIGURE 8-1 The Top Free area of the Apps page displays the most highly rated free apps.

4. Tap Facebook for Android.

5. Tap Download or Free depending on the Droid you have.

6. Tap Accept & Download or OK depending on the Droid you have.

7. The Status bar alerts you when the Facebook app successfully installed. You can view the Facebook app in the All Apps or Applications screen, as shown in Figure 8-2. (You may need to scroll through your apps to find it.)

Logging In

Now that Facebook is installed, it's time to log into Facebook so that you can sync your friends with your Contacts, view your news feeds, and more, which this chapter covers later. To begin follow these steps:

1. Tap the Facebook app. The Facebook login page appears, as shown in Figure 8-3.

2. Type the login email address in the Email box.

3. Type the password in the Password box.

4. Tap Login.

FIGURE 8-2 The Facebook app displays in the All Apps screen.

FIGURE 8-3 Type your email and password on the Faceboom login page.

WHAT IF I DON'T HAVE A FACEBOOK ACCOUNT? If you don't have a Facebook account before you use Facebook, tap the Sign Up link below the Login button. After you sign up, you can log in and start exploring.

Syncing Your Friends with Contacts

After you log in, the Sync Friends with Contacts screen, as shown in Figure 8-4, enables you to add your friends' Facebook pictures, your current status, and your contact information to your Contacts. You won't see this screen if you've used this app before on another Droid device, already set up Facebook with your Droid, or met other criteria in which this task has already been completed.

Follow these steps to sync your Facebook friend information with your Contacts:

1. Tap Sync All to sync all your friends' data with your Contacts.

2. Sync with Existing Contacts is selected by default; this option enables you to sync data only about your Facebook friends who are already in your contacts.

3. Tap Don't Sync to use information about friends only in Facebook, not in your Contacts.

4. Tap Finish.

5. Tap Not Now to put finding friends on Facebook on the back burner, which is discussed later.

FIGURE 8-4 You can sync your Facebook friends with your contacts on the Sync Friends with Contacts screen.

VIEWING THE NEWS FEED

The news feed from your friends appears after you set up Facebook. A news feed is the nerve center of Facebook, so you can get updated information from all your Facebook friends in real time in one place. The feed is categorized into eight different views that filter the feed by what's in each update. For example, you can view feeds that have only photos included. Most Recent is the default view.

Follow these steps to view and change the news feed:

1. Tap the Facebook bar at the top of the screen and then tap News Feed if necessary.

2. Tap Most Recent.

3. Scroll through the news feed category list, as shown in Figure 8-5, to find the view you want. Views range from Top News to Videos.

4. Tap the news feed you want to view.

5. Tap the plus (+) icon to open the pop-up bar so that you can either Like the news item or Comment on the news item.

6. Tap the Like/Comment bar below the news item to view who likes the news item and any comments about the news item.

FIGURE 8-5 Choose the news feed you want to view

FINDING AND CONTACTING YOUR FRIENDS

Naturally, one thing you'll want to do after you install the Facebook app is to find other people on Facebook who you want to add to your Friends list. You can find a friend in your Contact list easily using the Find Friends screen. This is a great option when you want to send a direct message to friends or access their page without scrolling through the status pages to locate their last post.

Follow these steps to find your friends and see what they're up to:

1. On the News Feed screen, tap the Back button.

2. Tap Friends, as shown in Figure 8-6.

FIGURE 8-6 Tap the Friends icon to manage your friend list.

3. In the Find Friends screen, as shown in Figure 8-7, type the name of a friend in the search box or scroll down the Friends list to find the friend.

FIGURE 8-7 The Find Friends screen displays a list of all your Facebook friends, so you can find the friend you need.

4. Tap the friend's name in the list. The latest update from your friend appears at the top of the update list on his Wall, as shown in Figure 8-8.

FIGURE 8-8 Your friend's Wall shows the update list with the latest update at the top of the list.

5. Send a note to your friend and others to see by typing your note in the Write Something box and then tapping Share.

6. Scroll down the list of Wall updates to view your friend's status updates. The most recent update is listed first. Like or Comment about your friend's status by tapping the status update and then tapping Like or writing the comment in the Write a Comment box.

7. Tap Info to view information about your friend, as shown in Figure 8-9.

8. Tap Email to send your friend a private email message.

9. View your friend's photos on his profile by tapping Photos. Figure 8-10 shows that your friend's photos are categorized as he chooses.

10. View a photo by tapping the category and then tapping the photo in the thumbnail list. When the photo appears on the screen, you can tap the Comment icon to send your friend a note about the photo.

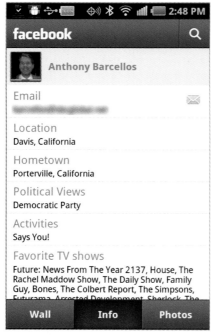

FIGURE 8-9 Read information about your friend in the Info screen.

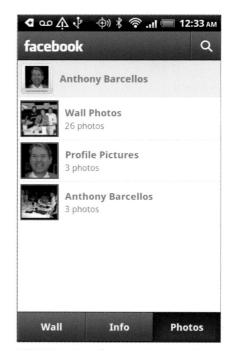

FIGURE 8-10 In this example, Eric's friend, Tony, has three photo categories.

SHARING STATUS UPDATES AND PHOTOS

You can easily share different types of status updates with your Facebook friends through your profile. For example, you may want to just type a text message. If you want your Facebook friends to get a better idea of what you did by sharing a photo, you can also easily add a photo to your status update.

Follow these steps to share text and photo status reports:

1. In the News Feed screen, press the Back button until you see the Facebook screen.

2. Tap Profile.

3. On the Profile page, as shown in Figure 8-11, type your update in the What's on Your Mind? box and then tap Share.

4. Upload a photo by tapping the Camera icon to the left of the What's on Your Mind? box and then tapping Photo.

5. Choose a photo from the Gallery on your Droid or take a photo using the on-board camera. You'll learn how to take pictures using the camera in Chapter 9 ("How do I Best Take, View, Share, and Manage Photos?").

6. After you select or take a photo, add a caption, as shown in Figure 8-12, and then tap Upload. Your photo caption appears on the top of your Wall for all your Facebook friends to see.

FIGURE 8-11 Eric's profile page displays his most recent status updates.

FIGURE 8-12 You can add a caption to your photo.

Integrating with Twitter

When I talk to people about Twitter, some of them shake their heads and wonder why it's so important—let alone popular. After all, a site that enables you to send messages that have only 140 or fewer characters isn't that effective, is it?

There's much more to Twitter than just the ability to send short messages. The experience is about following other Twitter users and having those users follow you. That encourages you and others to keep "tweeting" messages. You can set up a list of tweets based on a specific topic. You can search for trends. And Twitter has also set up apps on mobile devices so that you can tweet your followers and get tweets from others you follow.

That includes Android, too, and it's easy to find the Twitter app in the Android market and download it. Like the Facebook app, the Twitter app is free to download and use.

DOWNLOADING THE TWITTER ANDROID APP

Like the Facebook app, it's easy to download the Twitter app from the Android Market. After you download the app, the Droid installs Twitter automatically so that you go from download straight to sign in.

Start with learning how to download and then install the Twitter app:

1. Tap Market and then tap Apps.

2. At the top of the Apps page, flick left to the Top Free page (refer to Figure 8-1). In the Droid Incredible 2, scroll down, tap Social, and then tap Top Free.

3. Scroll down the page if necessary, and tap Twitter.

4. Tap Download or Free depending on the Droid you have.

5. Tap Accept & Download or OK depending on the Droid you have.

6. The status bar alerts you when the Facebook app successfully installs. You can view the Twitter app in the All Apps or Applications screen, as shown in Figure 8-13.

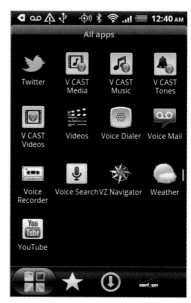

FIGURE 8-13 The Twitter app on the All Apps screen appears.

Sign In

Now that the Droid has installed the app, it's time to open Twitter, sign into your account, and start tweeting. If you already have an existing account and you can't sign in, it may be that you typed your username or password incorrectly; you won't get an error message saying so. That is, you just won't be moved from the Sign In screen. So, if the Twitter app seems to be stuck, double-check what you typed.

WHAT IF I DON'T HAVE A TWITTER ACCOUNT? Like Facebook, you can sign up for a free Twitter account by tapping the Sign Up button, which appears directly below the Sign In button.

Follow these steps to sign in on the Sign In screen:

1. Access the Twitter mobile website, as shown in Figure 18-14. If you like, you can choose to browse for a topic or name that you want to follow first.

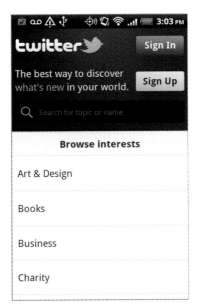

FIGURE 8-14 You can sign into or sign up for a Twitter account.

2. Sign in by tapping Sign In.

3. On the Sign In page, type your username or email address and your password; then tap Sign In. The Twitter screen shows your most recent tweets.

TWEETING MESSAGES

Now that you've taken care of all that setup and signup stuff, it's time for the fun part—tweeting messages to all your followers! A tweet is a short message sent to other Twitter users who are following you that tells them what's going on in your life. Because tweets are meant to be short, a character counter to the upper right of the box shows you how many more characters you have left available in your tweet. (As mentioned earlier, the maximum number of characters you have in a tweet is 140.)

If you don't have followers, you can start by typing a topic or name into the Search box to see what happens. For example, if you look for information about the city or town you live in, the search results may prompt you to start following people who live where you do.

Typing Text in Your Tweet

You can tweet anything you want to others; although, you should be mindful that if you tweet something that someone else finds offensive, Twitter may contact you soon to ask you to explain yourself. So here's how to tweet simple text messages:

1. Tap the Compose icon, as shown in Figure 8-15.

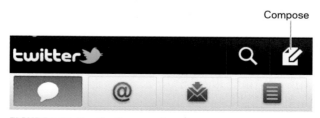

FIGURE 8-15 Tap the Compose icon to compose a tweet.

2. In the New Tweet screen, type in the What's Happening? box, as shown in Figure 8-16.

3. When you finish typing, tap Tweet. Your tweet appears in your tweet list.

Adding Photos to Your Tweet

People who aren't much into Twitter (or not into it at all) may not know that you can add a photo to your tweet to show (not just tell) your followers what you've been doing. When a follower reads the text tweet, Twitter automatically places a link to that photo within the tweet. When the user taps the link, the photo opens in the user's default photo viewer. To put a photo in your tweet, follow these steps:

1. In the New Tweet screen, tap the Photo icon, also shown in Figure 8-16.

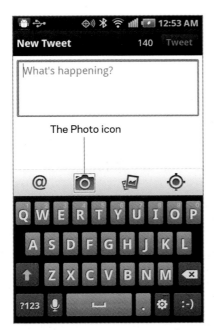

FIGURE 8-16 Type your tweet in the What's Happening? box.

2. Take your photo and then tap Done. You'll learn more about taking photos in Chapter 9 ("How do I Best Take, View, Share, and Manage Photos?").

3. Type the tweet in the What's Happening? box as you would for a normal tweet. The photo thumbnail appears below the box.

4. Tap Tweet. Your tweet appears in the tweet list and includes the link to the photo.

5. You can also tap the Photo and Video Album icon, as shown in Figure 8-17, to select a photo you've already taken that's stored in an album.

FIGURE 8-17 The Photo and Video Album icon displays.

All you have to do is tap an album in the Select an Album page and then tap the thumbnail image in the list. The image appears in the New Tweet page so that you can then compose your tweet.

Linking Videos to Your Tweet

Twitter doesn't host video files on its servers. Instead, Twitter did the smart thing by working with six different services, so when you view a tweet, you can see the video as well. Those services include the following:

+ YouTube
+ Vimeo
+ Ustream
+ Justin.tv
+ Twitlens
+ Twitvid

You can visit these sites to browse for the video you like. What's more, YouTube is pre-installed on your Droid, so you can access that site directly.

When you're in YouTube, you can share a video you're viewing by tapping Share and then tapping Twitter.

If you want to use another video service in the list, you can copy the web address of the video page you're viewing in the Browser from within the Address box and then paste it into the What's Happening box.

If you have the Browser open, all you must do is hold down the Home button in Twitter, open the Recent window, and then open the Browser window to access the video page. If you don't, you can access the Home screen after you hold the Home button and then tap Browser (or Internet), browse to the video site, and then open the video you want.

SENDING DIRECT MESSAGES

You may want to send a message to a follower without having all your followers read it. Instead of using email, you can do so using Twitter, which can be useful if you don't know the recipient's email address, or if the person you want to reach prefers Twitter over email.

You need to be on Twitter's main screen, so you can tap the icon to send a direct message. Follow these directions:

1. Tap the Envelope icon, as shown in Figure 8-18. A list of previous message threads appears on the page.

FIGURE 8-18 Click the Envelope icon to send a direct message.

2. Tap the Compose icon.

3. Tap New Message.

4. In the New Message screen, tap the plus button to the right of the To box, as shown in Figure 8-19, to select the follower to whom you want to send a message.

5. Find and tap the name of the follower.

6. Tap the Send a Message box.

7. Type the message in the box. The character counter appears in the upper-right corner of the box so that you know how many characters you have left to type in the message.

8. If you decide to send the message, tap Send. The message appears at the top of your message thread list.

9. If you decide not to send the message, press Back twice to return to your list of private messages. Return to your Twitter feed by tapping the icon that looks like a cartoon bubble.

FIGURE 8-19 Tap the plus button to select a recipient from the list.

HOW CAN I READ MESSAGES I'VE ALREADY SENT? After you tap the Envelope icon, a list of previous message threads appears on the page. The most recent message thread appears at the top of the list. Tap the message to view all the messages in the thread.

FOLLOWING YOUR FRIENDS

You can find friends on Twitter in two ways. One way is to search for a person's name in the Search box at the top of the Twitter page. Another is to tap Who to Follow and see people Twitter suggests you follow. If you already follow people, Twitter's suggestions are based on who you already follow. If you're not currently following anyone, Twitter gives you the chance to invite a follower by email.

Twitter also gives you other options to find friends in different interest categories, such as business and entertainment. With so many potential people
to follow (and many Twitter users follow large numbers of their fellow tweeters), you may want to take advantage of Twitter's suggestions. With all that
said, now look at how to use Twitter to follow your friends:

1. Tap the List icon, as shown in Figure 8-20. You can see this in various
   screens in this chapter, and it is to the right of the Envelope icon on the
   Twitter home screen.

2. Tap Suggested Users.

3. On the Suggested Users screen, tap the category that interests you.
   You may need to scroll down the list to find the category you want.

4. In the list of recent tweets from different technology tweeters, tap the
   Accounts icon, as shown in Figure 8-21.

5. In the list of Twitter users in your category, tap the user you want to follow.

6. Tap Follow.

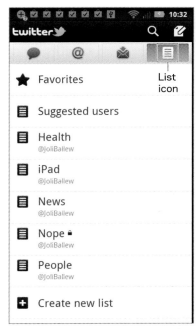

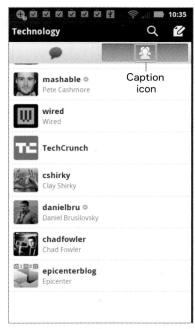

FIGURE 8-20 Tap the List icon on the
Twitter home screen.

FIGURE 8-21 Tap the Accounts icon for a
list of Twitter users to follow.

SEARCHING FOR INFORMATION

Though Twitter makes it easy for you to get information, sometimes you need to look for something specific on the site, such as a topic, an interest category, and a specific user on the site. In that case, Twitter's Search feature is for you. Here's how to use it:

1. On any Twitter screen, tap the Search icon, as shown in Figure 8-22.

2. In the Search screen, type the topic or name to search for in the Search for Topic or Name box.

FIGURE 8-22 Tap the Search icon to search for specific information.

3. Twitter displays a list of tweets with topics or names that match your search parameters. If the tweet is abridged in the list, tap the tweet to view it in its entirety.

Using Friend Stream for HTC Droid Incredible 2

Only the Droid Incredible 2 contains a nice app called Friend Stream. This app syncs your social network sites so that you can get updates from your friends on a regular basis without having to check social networking sites. All the updates from all your synced social media sites appear in aggregated form within the Friend Stream window. You can access Friend Stream from the Home screen or from the All Apps screen. You can learn more about how to use Friend Stream online at the book's website at www.wiley.com/go/ droidcompanion.

I SEE FEEDS AND UPDATES ON THE DROID CHARGE. IS IT THE SAME AS FRIEND STREAM? Feeds and Updates on the Droid Charge is similar to Friend Stream for the Droid Incredible 2. The Feeds and Updates app is also on a Home screen, and you set it up by tapping on the app window and then selecting the social networking sites you want to sync. There are also differences in the types of social network sites and the auto refresh times in Feeds and Updates.

Related Questions

✚ How do I use the phone and add contacts? **PAGE 68**

✚ How do I get the most from the Android Market? **PAGE 120**

✚ How do I take, view, share, and manage photos? **PAGE 216**

✚ How do I take, view, share, and play music and video? **PAGE 246**

✚ How do I use the Droid to more efficiently communicate and work? **ONLINE AT www.wiley.com/go/droidcompanion**

CHAPTER NINE

HOW DO I BEST TAKE, VIEW, SHARE, AND MANAGE PHOTOS?

In This Chapter:

+ Taking and Saving Photos
+ Using the Gallery App
+ Sharing Photos

Taking and Saving Photos

Nearly all smartphones available today have a digital camera included with the unit, and people not only snap photos and send them to others while on the go, they also send them to their friends on social networking sites such as Facebook, or even to a local TV news station.

Your Droid phone is no different. Most versions of the Droid contain cameras on the front and back of the unit. Some Droid models, such as the Droid X2, offer cameras only on the back. Whatever model you have, the Droid has the Camera app pre-installed so all you need to do is install your microSD card (the Droid stores photos on the card), open the app, view what the camera sees on the screen, point, and click. There's more you can do than just that in the Camera app, of course, but start off with the point-and-click basics and then delve deeper into the finer points to use the app.

ACCESSING THE CAMERA

You can access the Camera app in two ways. Depending on how you set up your Home screens, you can flick left or right to open the Home screen that contains the Camera app icon. You can also open the All Apps screen and then tap the Camera app, as shown in Figure 9-1. Of course, you can add the Camera icon to any Home screen or the Dock.

After you open the app, you see that the screen shows you what the camera sees through its lens. As you move around, the picture changes just as with any other camera. You can see a number of controls and other information on

FIGURE 9-1 The Camera app on the Droid Incredible 2 All Apps screen displays.

the screen as well. This information can include the following, depending on your Droid model:

+ The resolution of your camera, such as 8 megapixels on the Droid Charge

+ Battery life remaining on your Droid

+ The remaining number of pictures available on your microSD card

+ Settings menu bar

+ Zoom bar

+ Button so you can switch between the front and back camera, if a front-facing camera is available

+ Bar that enables you to take photos, view photos you've taken, and switch between the camera and video recorder

Depending on your Droid and how you hold it, you can see controls on the top and bottom of the screen. As you can see in Figure 9-2, the controls may appear sideways when held in the vertical view. The default horizontal view is shown in Figure 9-3.

You can rotate the unit horizontally and vertically, and the picture on your camera changes accordingly. That is, if you hold the unit vertically and rotate it 90 degrees while keeping the camera pointed at the same spot, you see more in your picture on the left and right sides of the screen.

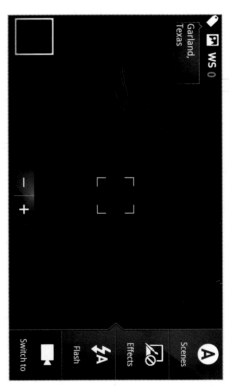

FIGURE 9-2 The vertical view on the Droid X2 appears with controls and in various places on the screen.

FIGURE 9-3 The default horizontal view on the Droid Charge appears with controls and other information at the left and right sides of the screen.

WILL THE CAMERA CONTROLS CHANGE IF I ROTATE THE UNIT? The location of the controls won't change, but how the controls appear on the screen depend on your Droid model. If you have the Droid Incredible 2 and rotate the unit 90 degrees to view the screen horizontally, you see the labels on the controls rotate as well. If you have a Droid Charge, Droid X2, or Droid 3, the labels don't change—you should take pictures in horizontal view.

TAKING A PICTURE

You can take a picture of something that appears behind the phone on just about any Droid phone, and you can take pictures of something that appears in front of the phone, such as your face, on phones with front-facing cameras. You can switch camera lenses by tapping the appropriate icon on the screen. Figure 9-4 shows the icon to tap on the Droid 3.

Switch from back-
to front-facing lenses

FIGURE 9-4 The icon to switch from
the front to the back camera lenses
on the Droid 3 looks like this.

The camera on the front of the unit may be a bit harder to spot because it's
a dark dot on a black background. The camera dot appears at the top of the
unit. Depending on your Droid, the camera may appear on the left or on the
right, the latter of which is shown in Figure 9-5.

FIGURE 9-5 The front camera in the upper-right corner of the Droid
Incredible 2.

When you turn on the Camera app, the back camera is active by default. If
you want to switch between the front camera and the back camera, tap the
camera side Switch icon on the Camera screen (refer to Figure 9-4).

Unfortunately, the Camera app and the Droid unit don't tell you which
camera you're using, but there's an easy way around that. If you're not sure
what camera you're using, hold the unit up in front of your face. If you see
your face, you know that you're using the front camera.

I KEEP PRESSING ANOTHER BUTTON ON THE UNIT AND EXITING THE CAMERA APP. HOW CAN I PREVENT THIS? When you use the camera on your Droid, it's likely that you grip the unit more carefully than you would when doing other things on the phone. However, that extra grip could mean your fingers move over buttons on your Droid, and you inadvertently go to another screen. Some Droid models such as the Droid Charge have a feature to prevent this; other models such as the Droid Incredible 2, Droid X2, and Droid 3 don't—for reasons unknown.

On the Droid Charge, to disable other apps from opening, briefly press the Power button. You see the Lock icon appear in the upper-right corner of the screen, as shown in Figure 9-6. You can briefly press the Power button again to enable the buttons.

FIGURE 9-6 The lock icon tells you that all other buttons on the Droid Charge are disabled.

The disable feature doesn't prevent you from turning off the Droid Charge if you hold down the Power button for a few seconds as you always do. If you want to just turn off the screen instead, you can't do that from the Camera app: Press the Home button, and then briefly press the Power button.

Setting the Focus

When you turn on the Camera app, you see a "viewfinder" type of screen that many cameras use to help you focus. This includes an auto-finder rectangle in the center of the screen, so you can focus on the center of the object you want to photograph. See Figure 9-7 for an example.

When you move the unit around to see the object you want to take a picture of, the auto-finder turns off, meaning it changes from the completed square shown in Figure 9-7 to a square that does not have complete sides. As you slowly move the unit, the Droid senses that you may be getting close to an object and turns on the auto-finder. When you stop, the view of your object briefly turns fuzzy and then sharpens. This indicates that the camera has your object in sight and is ready to shoot your picture.

FIGURE 9-7 The auto-finder makes it easy for you to focus on an object.

- -

CAN I CHANGE THE LOCATION OF THE AUTO-FINDER RECTANGLE?
Yes, you can change the location by tapping on another area in the Camera screen on some Droid phones. On the Droid X2 and Droid 3, you must tap and drag. When you move the camera around, the auto-finder searches for objects in that area of the screen.

- -

Depending on your Droid model, you can open the Camera settings and view available focus options. Following are the steps for the Droid Charge and the Droid Incredible 2:

1. Tap the Right Arrow button, and then tap the Settings icon or press the Menu button on your phone, depending on your Droid model.

2. Scroll down to view the focus types in the menu, or tap the Focus Mode type depending on your Droid model.

3. The default is Auto Focus. On the Droid Charge, you must choose between three different focus types for taking your photo; on the Droid Incredible 2, Auto Focus and Face Detection focus are selected by default, as shown in Figure 9-8.

4. If you're taking a photo of people, the Camera app automatically recognizes faces and shows all the faces it recognizes in boxes. Then the Droid automatically focuses on those faces to get the clearest picture possible. (If you don't have any faces in your photo, the Droid won't do anything.) However, Face Detection focus is not selected by default on the Droid Charge, so following are the steps to set face detection:

   A. Tap the Right Arrow button, and then tap the Settings icon, as shown in Figure 9-9.

   B. In the settings menu, tap Auto Focus.

   C. In the Focus Mode screen, as shown in Figure 9-10, tap Face Detection.

   D. Tap in the area below the menu to close it. You can change the focus to another mode by tapping Face Detection in the Settings menu and then tapping Auto Focus or Macro.

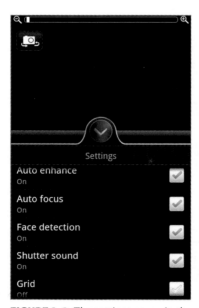

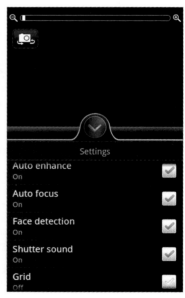

FIGURE 9-8 The settings menu in the Droid Incredible 2 shows that auto-focus and face detection focus are on.

FIGURE 9-9 The settings icon appears in the Droid Charge Camera's settings menu bar.

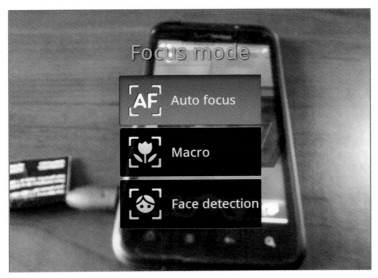

FIGURE 9-10 Tap Face Detection in the Focus Mode screen.

5. If you have a Droid Charge, you can also set the focus mode to Macro, which enables you to take focused pictures of small objects (such as a ladybug on a flower) at a close range. Follow these steps:

   A. Tap the Right Arrow button, and then tap the Settings icon (refer to Figure 9-10).

   B. On the Settings menu, tap Auto Focus.

   C. On the Focus Mode screen (refer to Figure 9-10), tap Macro.

   D. Tap in the area below the menu to close it. You can change the focus to another mode by tapping Face Detection in the Settings menu and then tapping Macro or Face Detection.

WHY DON'T I SEE THE AUTO-FINDER ON THE FRONT CAMERA?
Some Droid phones don't use the auto-finder on the front camera. You also can't zoom in and out of photos, use the flash, and use face detection on the front camera.

To access and configure settings on the Droid 3, with the back-facing camera selected, follow these steps:

1. Press the Menu button.

2. Tap the Settings icon on the far left, as shown in Figure 9-11. Tap to change the following:

   A. Whether the pictures should be taken in Widescreen mode.

   B. What video resolution you want to use.

   C. Where you want to store camera data.

   D. Whether you want to Geo-tag information. See Figure 9-12.

FIGURE 9-11 The Droid 3 offers a Settings icon on the screen, which you can access by pressing the Menu button.

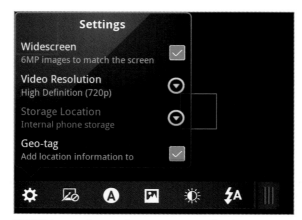

FIGURE 9-12 The Droid 3 Settings icon offers access to general settings.

3. Tap each subsequent icon:

   A. **Effects**—Sets Normal, Black and White, Negative, or Sepia

   B. **Scenes**—Sets Auto, Portrait, Landscape, Sport, Night Portrait, Sunset, Macro, or Steady Shot

   C. **Modes**—Sets Single Shot or Panorama

    D. Brightness—Sets the brightness of the shot

    E. Flash—Sets Flash Off, Flash On, or Auto Flash

SETTINGS DIFFER IF YOU CHOOSE THE FRONT-FACING CAMERA OR THE VIDEO CAMERA The options available in Settings on the Droid 3 differ if you do not set the back-facing camera, or if you select the video camera instead of the camera. On the Droid X2, the latter is also true. What you see when in the video camera differs from what you see in the still camera.

To access and configure settings on the Droid X2 with the back-facing camera selected, follow these steps:

1. Press the Menu button on the phone.

2. Tap Settings, as shown in Figure 9-13.

Picture modes   Tags   Settings

FIGURE 9-13 The Droid X2 Settings icon offers access to general settings.

3. Tap the following, as shown in Figure 9-14, to configure settings; you may have to scroll to access all the options:

    A. Picture Resolution—Changes from Widescreen to Large, Medium, Small, or Tiny

    B. Video Resolution—Changes from the default 320 x 240 to another option

    C. Exposure—Changes the exposure, which helps the camera lens take in more or less light than the default, to account for low or high light settings

    D. Shutter Tone—Enables or disables the sound the phone makes when you take a picture

E. **Storage Location**—Changes where data is saved by default

F. **Focus Options**—Changes from Continuous Focus (the default) to Auto Focus

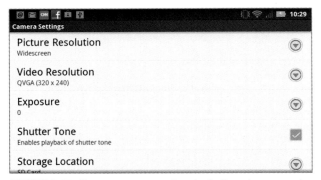

FIGURE 9-14 Change camera settings including picture resolution, video resolution, and more in the Camera Settings screen.

4. Press the Back button on your phone; press the Menu button on your phone.

5. Tap Picture Modes (refer to Figure 9-13).

6. Choose from Single Shot, Panorama, and Multi-Shot.

7. Press the Back button on your phone.

Zooming In and Out

You don't need to physically move to get a closer view of your object. This is useful if you're at a location that can't physically allow you to move closer (such as when you're close to nature and getting any closer might compromise your safety) or if you want to see how an object looks at close range. All the Droid models we've seen have a zoom option, which either appears as a bar that you can drag or tap, or a − and + sign that you tap to zoom.

✦ On the Droid 3 and Incredible 2, hold and drag the zoom bar to zoom in or out. You can also tap anywhere on the bar to zoom in or out to the zoom level that corresponds to that location on the bar.

- On the Droid Charge, simply pinch in and out on the Camera screen to zoom in and out, respectively.
- On the Droid X2, tap the – or + sign to zoom, as shown in Figure 9-15.

FIGURE 9-15 The Droid X2 offers + and – icons for zooming.

Setting Up the Flash

The Droid X2, Droid 3, and Droid Incredible 2 have auto-detect flash turned on by default. The Auto-Flash icon appears as an icon with a lightning bolt and the letter A, as shown in Figure 9-16. With this setting when you take a picture, the Droid determines if you don't have enough light in the area; if not, the Droid uses the flash to compensate. If you're uncertain about when to use a flash to take pictures, the auto-flash is best for you.

FIGURE 9-16 The Auto-Flash icon has a lightning bolt with the letter A to tell you the Camera will use the flash automatically if needed.

You can change the flash status to three different states when you tap the Auto-Flash icon. Tap the status once to turn the flash into an always-on state (a lightning bolt) and then tap it again to turn the flash off (a lightning bolt with a no sign on top of it). If you tap the Flash Off icon, you see the Auto-Flash icon and return to the third and default flash state. On the Droid 3 or the Droid X2, press the Menu button on the phone, and then tap the Flash icon to change the setting. You can also simply tap the screen to bring up these controls on either phone.

The Droid Charge, on the other hand, has the flash automatically turned off. The Flash Off icon has a lightning bolt with a line through it in the settings menu bar, as shown in Figure 9-17.

FIGURE 9-17 The Flash Off icon on the Droid Charge has a lightning bolt with a line through it to signify the flash is off.

You can change the flash setting by tapping the Flash Off icon in the settings bar and then selecting Off, On, or Auto Flash in the Flash menu. After you tap your selection, the icon changes on the Settings menu bar, and you return to the Camera screen.

Additional Settings

No matter what Droid model you have, you can apply more settings to the Camera app before you start shooting, so your photo will turn out just right.

As noted earlier for the Droid X2 and the Droid 3, you access the options by first pressing the Menu button. You explored those settings earlier. You also press the Menu button on the Incredible 2 to start. In the Droid Charge, open the Settings menu bar. If you haven't explored them yet, the options you see can include the following:

+ The shooting mode for the type of object you're photographing. For example, you can select the Add Me mode on the Droid Charge to combine people from a photo with another background.

+ Scene modes that tell the Camera app what type of picture you're taking so the app can modify the settings accordingly and (hopefully) give you the best picture for the scene you're shooting.

✦ The ability to adjust your photo resolution. Your resolution range depends on your Droid model.

✦ Enhance the LCD visibility on your Droid when you take photos outdoors.

WHAT HAPPENS TO THE CAMERA WHEN YOU PUT THE DROID DOWN? If you have the Camera app open and you put the Droid down on a desk to do something else, what happens next depends on the Droid you use. After 30 seconds or so, the Droid Charge thinks that you don't want to use the camera and returns to the previous page, such as the Apps or Home page. The Droid 3 returns to the Home screen in even less time. The Droid X2 doesn't seem to automatically ever turn the camera off. On the Droid Incredible 2, a message appears that asks you to tap the screen to activate the camera. On any Droid model, the entire display screen turns off per your screen settings, and you must restart the Camera app again when this happens.

SHOOT YOUR PHOTO AND ADD EFFECTS

Now that you've finished reviewing and setting up your photo settings, it's time to do the most important thing—take a picture! Doing this is easy: Just point and press the Shutter icon, as shown in Figure 9-18. Depending on the Droid model you use, the icon may look like what's in the figure or may have the picture of a camera.

When you take a photo, the Droid makes a sound like a camera whirring, which is a sound left over from the days of film cameras. That sound tells you that the Droid has successfully taken the photo. (You may also see visual features such as the light of the flash going off.)

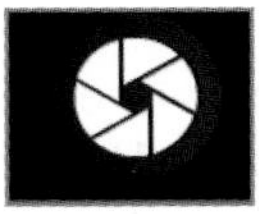

FIGURE 9-18 Tap the Shutter icon to take the picture.

Adding Effects

The type of Droid you have determines what sort of options you have available to tweak your pictures. These options don't replace Photoshop by any means, but if you don't need something that complicated, the settings that the Camera app provides may be just what you need.

In the Droid X2, Droid 3, and Incredible 2, you access the options by pressing the Menu button. In the Droid Charge, you open the Settings menu bar (refer to Figure 9-9). Options can include the following:

+ Applying different effects such as sepia tones, grayscale (and thus removing color) from your photo, and changing your photo into a bunch of dots

+ Changing the image quality, including exposure, contrast, sharpness, and saturation of your photo

+ Changing the white balance in your photo to make it look cloudy, in daylight, fluorescent, or incandescent

+ Changing the exposure value of your photos

REVIEW YOUR PHOTO AND TELL THE DROID WHAT TO DO WITH IT

After you take a picture, the Camera app automatically saves the picture to your microSD card. From here, you can manipulate the photo.

Droid X2 and Droid 3

With the Droid X2 and Droid 3 you can edit pictures you've taken through the Review menu bar, as shown in Figure 9-19.

FIGURE 9-19 The Review menu bar enables you to determine what happens to your photo.

To get here on the Droid X2 and the Droid 3, follow these steps:

1. Open the picture by tapping it in the Camera app or by locating it in the Gallery.

2. Press the Menu button on the phone.

3. Tap Edit to access options such as Rotate, Crop, and Advanced Editing (which takes you to a screen where you can enhance the photo in many ways: rotate it, add effects, and more).

Droid Incredible 2

On the Droid Incredible 2, the four icons on the menu bar, as shown in Figure 9-20, enable you to do the following:

1. Return to the viewfinder so that you can take another photo.

2. Delete the photo from the microSD card.

3. Share the photo with your computer or another phone; you can also send the photo to someone else by email or post it on a social networking site.

4. Set the photo as another type of graphic on your phone such as a Contact icon or your Home screen wallpaper.

This menu quickly disappears and you can't get it back, so if you don't see the menu, you can manipulate the photo in the Gallery app discussed later in this chapter.

FIGURE 9-20 The Droid Incredible 2 menu bar shows four different options after you take a photo.

FIGURE 9-21 The small thumbnail of the photo you just took appears below the Photo icon, so you can tap it and manipulate it.

Droid Charge

The Droid Charge shows a small thumbnail version of your photo below the Photo icon, as shown in Figure 9-21. Tap this thumbnail photo to open it to determine what you want to do with it.

The menu appears at the bottom of the screen; so you can manipulate it. You can do three things in this menu, follow these steps:

1. Share the picture via a wide variety of methods including a Bluetooth connection, posting

the photo on Picasa, sending the photo by email or IM, and posting the message on a social networking site.

2. Set the photo as a Contact icon or your Home screen wallpaper.

3. Delete the photo from the microSD card.

If you don't see the menu, just tap the photo. The menu disappears after a few seconds, but you can bring it back by tapping the photo again.

Using the Gallery App

The Camera app gives you a few methods for manipulating your photos, but if you want more functionality, use the pre-installed Gallery app. You can't access the Gallery app from the Home screen (unless you decide to move it there, that is), so you need to tap the Gallery icon in the All Apps or Applications screen. When there you can view all your photos and select individual photos as necessary to work with them. Like the Camera app, the Gallery app works one way for the Droid X2 and Droid 3, another for the Droid Charge, and yet another for the Droid Incredible 2.

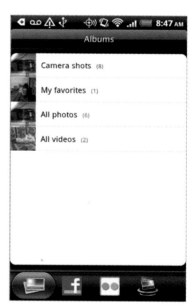

BROWSING FOLDERS IN THE DROID INCREDIBLE 2

The Droid Incredible 2 has two default folders: Camera Shots and All Photos. Unless you've added photos or videos from another source, the number of photos in the Camera Shots and All Photos albums is the same, as shown in Figure 9-22.

After you tap the album or folder name, the presentation of the photos in the list also differs. The Droid Incredible 2 shows a filmstrip of your photos (refer to Figure 9-23) if you hold your phone in

FIGURE 9-22 The Albums page contains the default Camera Shots and All Photos folders, and the Camera Shots folder contains all files in the All Photos and All Videos folders.

horizontal view. If you hold the phone in vertical view, you see thumbnail versions of your pictures arranged in a grid.

FIGURE 9-23 A filmstrip of your photos displays in horizontal view, so you can flick to the left and right to see your photos.

You can view the photo settings bar by pressing the Menu button. The icons in the bar vary depending on what you installed on your Droid, but your options may include the following:

+ Set your photo as a different type of graphic, such as background wallpaper.

+ Run a slideshow; you learn about slideshows later in this chapter.

+ Select the player for your slideshow.

+ Show where the photo was taken in the Maps app. The location is an approximation, but you can get a sense of where the address is.

+ View details about the photo, including the filename and path, the file type, and the GPS location that tells you where the photo was taken.

BROWSING FOLDERS IN THE DROID CHARGE

The Droid Charge shows you a thumbnail list of your photos. When you tap a photo, you see the full-screen version of that photo. You can flick to the left and right to move between photos in the Camera folder, and the folder information at the upper left of the screen tells you what photo you're on, as shown in Figure 9-24.

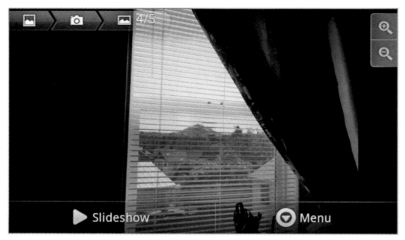

FIGURE 9-24 Flick between photos to view them in the folder; the folder information at the upper-left portion of the screen shows the fourth of five photos in the folder.

CAN I ADD FOLDERS AND CHANGE FOLDER NAMES? Yes, but you need to do so by connecting your Droid to your computer and having your computer recognize your Droid as a hard drive. Then you can go into your computer's file explorer, navigate to the directory that contains your folders (for example, /DCIM/) and then add folders and change folder names. The next time you open the Gallery, you see your changes reflected on the screen.

BROWSING FOLDERS IN THE DROID X2 AND DROID 3

When you open the Gallery in the Droid X2 or the Droid 3, you see the options shown in Figure 9-25. You can flick left and right on the thumbnails shown toward the top of this image, or you can tap any section to enter it and see photos there.

FIGURE 9-25 Tap any item here to enter a new view; Camera Roll lets you access the photos you've taken with your Droid's camera.

The folders on the Droid X2 and Droid 3 include the following:

✚ **Camera Roll**—Tap Camera Roll to view photos (and videos) you've taken with your camera. This is where you can tap to get to a photo you want to edit. (Tap the Back button to return to the screen shown in Figure 9-25.)

✚ **My Library**—Tap to see pictures (and videos) in your personal library. These may come via syncing with your computer, saving from an email, or other sources.

✚ **Online**—Tap to view photos you store online or have access to online from places such as Facebook.

✦ **Friends**—Tap to see related Friends lists, such as friends you have on Facebook. You can tap any friend to see related online photos.

✦ **DLNA servers**—Tap to see photos and videos on media servers you have access to. You need to tap to connect. See Figure 9-26.

FIGURE 9-26 DLNA lets you access media on shared network computers as well as share what's on your phone with them .

MOVING BETWEEN FOLDERS ON THE DROID CHARGE AND DROID INCREDIBLE 2

All the Droid models covered in this book make it easy for you to move between folders even when you're looking at photos. On the Droid X2 and the Droid 3, you simply flick left or right while in any folder or view. However, what you see and how you move been folders differs for the Incredible 2 and the Charge.

Droid Incredible 2

When you view a filmstrip or grid of photos in the Droid Incredible 2, you see a photo menu bar at the bottom of the screen. Tap the Albums icon, which has three horizontal lines and is located at the far left of the menu bar, as shown in Figure 9-27.

FIGURE 9-27 The Albums icon displays in the photo menu bar.

After you tap the Albums icon, the Albums screen appears again, so you can tap another album in the list.

Droid Charge

When you view a photo, tap it to open the menus at the top and bottom of the list. The top menu in the upper-left corner of the screen is the folder menu and shows you the three folders as buttons, as shown in Figure 9-28. When you tap these buttons, you go to a different folder or get more information about the photo.

Following are these buttons, from left to right:

✦ The Home button takes you to the Gallery Home page.

✦ The Camera button takes you to the Camera directory page with the thumbnail images.

✦ The total number of photos in the folder and where the photo you're viewing resides in the folder list. For example, if you view the first of five photos, you see 1/5. If you tap this button, you see the picture filename.

FIGURE 9-28 The directory menu
contains three directory icons so that
you know where you are in the Gallery.

EDITING PHOTOS

After you open a photo, the Gallery app has some basic tools so that you can
edit the photo. For example, you may want to crop a photo so that a photo
you share with others shows only the one object you want people to focus on.

You can't edit a photo without opening it to full size. On the Droid 2, Droid
X3, and Droid Incredible 2, you can open a photo in vertical view by tapping
the thumbnail photo in the grid; in horizontal view you can double-tap the
photo in the filmstrip. On the Droid Charge, you tap the thumbnail photo in
the Camera folder.

After you open the folder, tap the photo to open the photo menu bar at
the bottom of the screen. Depending on which Droid model you have, tap
the Magic Wand icon, or tap Menu and then tap More. On the Droid X2 and
Droid 3, press the Menu button. You see the Edit Photo menu, as shown in
Figure 9-29.

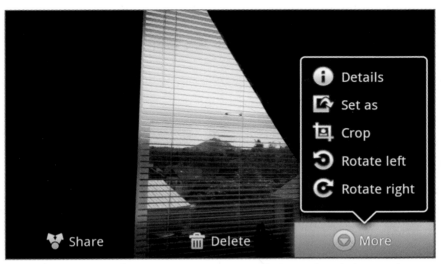

FIGURE 9-29 The Edit Photo menu on the Droid Charge shows a list of editing tools, ways to get details about the photo, and how you can set the photo as another graphic type.

The following editing options may be available depending on your Droid model:

+ **Details**—The details about the photo, including the filename, the file type, and when the photo was taken.

+ **Set As**—Set the photo as background wallpaper for your Home screen or as your Contact icon.

+ **Crop**—Crop the photo by moving and resizing the bounding box around the area you want to keep in the photo.

+ **Effects**—Apply effects to the photo from Auto-Enhance to sharpen the photo to Antique to give the photo an antique feel. The default is No Effect.

+ **Rotate Left**—Rotate the photo 90 degrees counterclockwise.

+ **Rotate Right**—Rotate the photo 90 degrees clockwise.

You can close the Edit Photo menu by tapping or pressing the Back button or by tapping elsewhere on the photo.

The Droid X2 and the Droid 3 offer many other editing options. To see these options, open any photo from the Gallery; then press the Menu button on your phone. Note the options to Edit, Delete, Add to Album, Set As, and More. More offers the option to create a slideshow, print, get picture info, and so on. If you tap Edit, you can rotate and crop or tap Advanced Editing. Refer to Figure 9-19 to see advanced editing options.

Sharing Photos

After you take your photos and they look the way you want, the Droid gives you the ability to share your photos both privately and publicly. You can do the following:

+ Move the photos to your computer using a Bluetooth connection.
+ Move the photos to other applications such as Picasa.
+ Share the photos wirelessly with other media players such as a television.
+ Send a photo by email or IM.
+ Post a photo online to social networking sites, including Facebook, Twitter, and Flickr.

You can also share one photo that you view in full-screen mode or select one or more photos in your album or folder.

EMAILING PHOTOS

As you learned in Chapter 6 ("How Do I Get the Most from Messaging, Chats, and Email?"), all models of the Droid come with two email programs built in: the Mail (or Email) app and the Gmail app. For the purpose of this chapter, take a look at how to email one or more photos using the Gmail app.

Email a Single Photo

To email a single photo that you view in full-screen mode, follow these steps:

1. Tap the photo to open the photo menu bar, and then press Menu if necessary.

2. Tap Share. Generally, this looks like a circle with two arrows sticking out of the top of it.

3. Tap Gmail. A new message appears on the Compose screen ready for you to add the recipient, subject name, and your message. The photo is attached to the message, as shown in Figure 9-30.

4. After you compose your message, tap the Send button in the upper-right corner of the Compose screen.

FIGURE 9-30 A new message on the Gmail Compose screen shows the file-name of the photo you can send.

Email Multiple Photos

To email one or multiple photos from an album or folder on the Droid Incredible 2 and Droid Charge, follow these steps:

1. Open the photo album or Camera folder, depending on your Droid model.

2. If you use a Droid Incredible 2, go to step 4.

3. If you have a Droid Charge, tap and hold down your finger on the first photo you want to send. Then select the photos you want to send by tapping each photo. When you do, the checkmark in the upper-right corner of the photo turns green. You can also select all the photos in the folder by tapping Select All.

4. Tap Share and then tap Gmail. If you have a Droid Charge, go to step 6.

5. If you have a Droid Incredible 2, select the photos you want to send by tapping each photo. When you do, the checkmark in the upper-left corner of the photo turns green.

6. After you select the photos, tap Next.

7. A new message appears on the Compose screen ready for you to add the recipient, subject name, and your message (refer to Figure 9-30). The only difference is that the message shows the multiple messages you selected.

8. When you finish composing your message, tap the Send icon in the upper-right corner of the Compose screen.

WATCH YOUR ATTACHMENT SIZE LIMITS Gmail has a maximum message size limit of 25MB, which is more than enough for sending and receiving photos in most cases. However, you can send a message up to only 25MB to another Gmail user. If you try to send a large message to a user who isn't using Gmail, both you and the recipient are subject to the maximum message size limit of the recipient's email service. Therefore, be sure to know what email service your recipient uses and the maximum message size.

To send multiple photos in an email on the Droid X2 or the Droid 3, follow these steps:

1. Open Camera Roll or My Library from the Gallery. (Later you can experiment with other folders.)

2. Press the Menu button and tap Select Multiple.

3. Tap to select the photos to send. See Figure 9-31.

FIGURE 9-31 When you select multiple photos, green checks appear by the ones you've selected.

4. Press the Menu button and tap Share.

5. Tap Email or Gmail. Note the other options.

6. Complete as necessary.

Related Questions

✦ How do I get the most from messaging and email? **PAGE 140**

✦ How do I best take, view, share, and play music and video? **PAGE 246**

✦ How do I use the Droid to communicate and work more efficiently?
ONLINE AT www.wiley.com/go/droidcompanion

CHAPTER TEN

HOW DO I BEST TAKE, VIEW, SHARE, AND PLAY MUSIC AND VIDEO?

In This Chapter:

+ Copying and Downloading Music
+ Playing Music
+ Creating Playlists
+ Buying Music and Media Online
+ Listening to Audiobooks, Podcasts, and Other Audible Files
+ Taking, Saving, and Sharing Video
+ Using the Video App
+ Editing Videos

I n this chapter you learn how to obtain music, play that music, and manipulate the music you've stored (or have access to) on your Droid phone. This may involve syncing music from a PC, downloading it from the web, or subscribing to a music service. After you're familiar with playing that music with the Music app, you learn how to use the Droid's camcorder, use the Video app to view your video, and share your video with other people. Start by looking at your options to get music on your Droid phone.

Copying and Downloading Music

You can get music on your smartphone using many techniques. As you learned in Chapter 2 ("How do I Make the Droid Uniquely Mine?"), if you have music on your personal computer, you can sync your music with Media Player on a Windows PC using a USB cable, and you can open the DLNA app, connect to your music over your wireless network, and copy it. You can even drag and drop your music files if you understand your Droid's file structure. If you haven't done any of this yet, a few of the options are briefly mentioned here so that you can start. When you have the time, return to Chapter 2 for the full story.

If you don't have music to copy from your own PC, you can download music directly to your Droid from the pre-installed V CAST app that gives you the option to sign up to the Rhapsody music service to get unlimited music downloads for a monthly fee. You can also download music from other sources on the web, using varying techniques and applications, which you can explore.

Whatever the case, after you have access to the music you want on your phone, you can use the Music app or Music Player to play it. On the Droid X2, Droid 3, and Droid Incredible 2, the Music app is likely already on a Home screen. On the Droid Charge, the Music app is called Music Player and it's in the Applications window.

- -

WHERE IS MY MUSIC STORED? When you finish copying or downloading music, the Droid stores the files on the phone's microSD card. The Music app or Music Player automatically recognizes these music files, so when you use these apps, you can select a song and immediately play it. Because the music is stored on the SD card, you may connect the phone to your computer, access this card from Computer or My Computer on your PC, and drag and drop files there to copy them.

- -

COPY MUSIC FROM YOUR COMPUTER

If you have music stored on your computer and you want to copy it to your Droid's microSD card, it's easy to do. However, you must have previously connected your phone and installed the proper device drivers so that your computer recognizes the phone and communicates with it. If you've done that, on any Droid phone, do the following:

1. Connect your USB cable to your computer.

2. If necessary, tap Disk Drive on the Connect to PC screen, and then tap Done.

3. Navigate to the Droid's external storage area using your computer's file explorer, such as Windows Explorer on a PC (shown in Figure 10-1) or Mac Finder on an Apple computer. You must access the wanted folder by opening the parent folder and then opening any resulting subfolders.

4. Position the Explorer or Finder to take up half the screen; position your music folder on your computer to take up the other half. Then:

   A. On the Droid X2 and Droid 3, drag music files from your computer to the Music folder (Open Media; then Music).

   B. On the Droid Incredible 2, copy to the download directory.

   C. On the Droid Charge, copy to the Playlists directory.

5. When you finish, disconnect your phone from your computer.

FIGURE 10-1 The Music directory on your Droid appears in your file explorer.

SYNC TO A MEDIA PLAYER

If you have a lot of music stored on your preferred media player on your computer, such as Windows Media Player or iTunes, you can sync directly to that player when you connect your Droid. Here's what each Droid model does when you connect your computer to the Droid with your USB cable.

Droid Charge

If you have a Droid Charge and you want to sync to a media player, you need to download a media sync app from the Android Market. Fortunately, there are good, free apps available. For example, you can download Winamp to sync with Windows Media Player or doubleTwist to sync with iTunes. Of course, if you have a Droid model other than a Charge, you can also use these apps. Go back to Chapter 5, "How Do I Get the Most from the Android Market?," for more information about downloading apps from the Market.

Droid Incredible 2

Your Droid Incredible 2 asks you how you want to connect to your PC. Tap Media Sync, as shown in Figure 10-2, and then tap Done.

Droid X2 or Droid 3

To get to a similar screen on your Droid X2 or Droid 3, pull down on the Status bar after your phone connects to your computer, and tap USB Connection. From there, you can choose Windows Media Sync and tap OK. (The actual syncing process is outlined in Chapter 2, but you may figure it out from here; on a PC, open Windows Media Player to start.)

When you connect a Droid X2 or a Droid 3, you won't be prompted by your phone on how to connect, but you may be prompted by your computer. If you installed the necessary drivers, you may even see

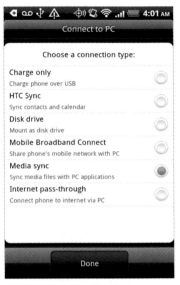

FIGURE 10-2 Tap Media Sync to sync your Droid with your computer's media player.

what's shown in Figure 10-3, provided you use Windows 7. Here, you can let the computer help you transfer files.

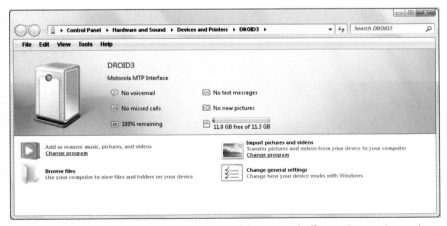

FIGURE 10-3 Windows 7 recognizes some Droid devices and offers assistance in syncing and transferring media.

Likewise, if your computer recognizes the new device and asks you what you want to do, as shown in Figure 10-4, you can select an option. In this example, you can click Sync Digital Media Files to This Device using Windows Media Player.

The Windows Media Player opens on your computer, so you can drag your songs to your sync list and then sync your music when you finish. Again, see Chapter 2 for more information.

DOWNLOAD MUSIC FROM A SERVICE

A number of free music services are available where you not only can download music from their database but also upload your own music to their web servers, so you can listen to your music on any computer or device you own. For example, you can add free music from Google's free Music Beta Magnifier site into your Google account and download that music using Google's free Music app, which you can download from the Android Market.

FIGURE 10-4 In the Windows AutoPlay window, sync digital media files using Windows Media Player.

- -

DO I NEED A GOOGLE ACCOUNT? If you want to use the Google Music Beta service, you need a Google account because the Music Beta service uploads music to your account, and the Music app downloads that music from your account.

- -

Before you download the Music app, you need to add music to your Google account so that the Music app can download it. You need to do this on a PC so that you can sign up for the service, and viewing the site on your PC monitor is much easier on the eyes.

1. Go to the Google Music Magnifier website at `http://magnifier` `.blogspot.com`.

2. Scroll down the page, and click Free Song Archive, as shown in Figure 10-5.

FIGURE 10-5 Click Free Song Archive to browse free libraries of songs in different genres.

3. Tap the genre name in the list.

4. Click Add Free Music, as shown in Figure 10-6.

5. Select the genre you want to listen to.

6. Click Add Free Music. See Figure 10-7.

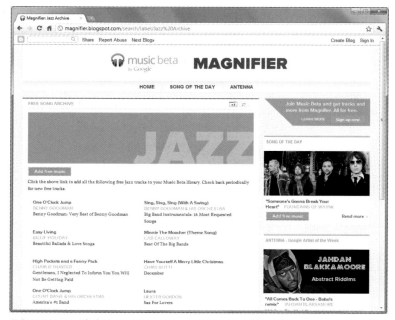

FIGURE 10-6 Click the Add Free Music button to select the genre you want to listen to after you review the list of songs.

FIGURE 10-7 Select one or more genres with songs you want to download to your Droid, and then click Add Free Music.

Now, to download the Music app, follow these steps:

1. Open the Android Market.

2. Search for Google Music Beta.

3. Tap Music in the Results screen.

4. Tap Download for Free.

5. Tap Accept & Download or OK.

6. After the app installs, you may need to tap the app name again to open the page. On the app page, tap Open.

If you have a Google account, the Music app invites you to link the Music app to Google Music, as shown in Figure 10-8.

To set up the Music app to sync with Google Music, follow these steps:

1. On the Welcome screen, tap Next.

2. The Music app links to your Google account. Tap Done.

3. The Music app shows the list of all the artists you downloaded in the genre (in this example, jazz) along with the other music you already downloaded that's stored on your Droid. See Figure 10-9.

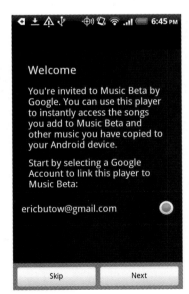

FIGURE 10-8 Select your Google account in the list if there is more than one, and then tap Next.

FIGURE 10-9 The list of downloaded music files from Google Music appears along with other music files you downloaded previously.

WHY DON'T I SEE ANY MUSIC ON MY DROID CHARGE? To view music playlists on your Droid Charge, you need to turn off USB storage by pulling down the Status bar and tapping Turn Off USB Storage. After you tap Stop, you see your music playlist.

The Google Music service isn't the only game in town. Simply search for **free music downloads** on your favorite search engine to see a long list of services that you can browse.

DOWNLOAD MUSIC FROM THE WEB

Though music catalog websites are great places to find the music you need, plenty of other sites post music on their sites as links, so you can play the music within your web browser or save the link to your computer. For the Droid, you can do the latter to save the music file to your Droid's microSD card. To do it, follow these steps:

1. Tap Browser (or Internet) on the Home screen.

2. Browse to a site that contains music such as www.mfiles.co.uk.

3. Hold down your finger on the link that you want to save.

4. In the menu that appears, tap Save Link. You can view the status of the download by pulling down the Status bar.

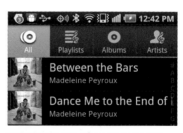

5. Press Home, and then tap Music (or Music Player) either on the Home screen or in the apps list.

6. The song appears on the screen, as shown in Figure 10-10. Tap the Music icon to begin playing the song.

FIGURE 10-10 The song appears on the Music screen; tap the Music icon to begin playing it.

Playing Music

After you finish syncing music and downloading music to your Droid, it's time to enjoy the playback of your music. If you don't have access to the Music app on your Home screen, place it there before moving forward. (On the Droid X2 or Droid 3, open All Apps, tap and hold the Music app, and tap Add to Home.)

PLAY IN THE MUSIC APP

To play music on the Droid X2 or Droid 3, follow these steps:

1. Open the Music app.

2. Tap the various tabs to explore the music on your Droid phone. See Figure 10-11.

3. Choose an artist, an album, a song, a playlist, or a genre.

4. Tap the wanted song to play it.

5. Note the controls, as shown in Figure 10-12, on the Droid X2. They include the following:

   A. Return to playlist or album view.

   B. Shuffle songs in the list.

   C. Repeat songs in the list.

   D. Start over.

   E. Play/Pause.

   F. Skip to the next song in the list.

   G. Slide to a new area of the song with the progress bar.

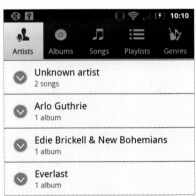

FIGURE 10-11 On the Droid X2 and the Droid 3, explore the tabs and tap any song to play it.

6. Press Menu to view more options, including but not limited to Audio Effects, Library, Add to Playlist, and Use as Ringtone.

Return to playlist or album view

Repeat songs in the list

Shuffle songs in the list

Skip to the next song in the list

Start over   Play/ Pause   Slide to a new area of the song with the progress bar

FIGURE 10-12 When a song is playing, you have access to several options to control it.

To play music on the Droid Incredible 2, follow these steps:

1. Tap Music on the Home screen.

2. If you can't access the music on the microSD card, pull down the Status bar, and change the USB connection type to something other than Disk Drive.

3. In the Music screen that appears, tap and hold on the Music icon for the song, and then flick left and right to move between songs.

4. At the top of the screen, note the icons and information for playing your music as shown in Figure 10-13, from left to right:

   A. Tap the Shuffle icon to shuffle playback of your songs in the queue.

   B. The Now Playing information shows you how many songs are in the queue and the song's place in the queue.

C. Tap the Sound Enhancer icon to add sound enhancements including audio enhancements created by SRS Labs and to apply an equalizer effect for listening through headphones.

D. Tap the Repeat icon to repeat the current song instead of moving to the next song in the queue after the song ends.

5. The playback timeline appears between the song title and the artist name.

6. In the bar at the bottom of the screen, note the icons you can tap:

Now playing
1 / 8

FIGURE 10-13 The icons and information at the top of the Music screen allow you to change how your Droid plays the current song in the queue.

A. Tap the Library icon to view music library information. See the next section.

B. Tap the left arrow to move back one song in the queue.

C. Tap the Play icon to play the song. After you tap this icon, it changes to a Pause icon (two parallel lines); you can pause playback by tapping the Pause icon.

D. Tap the right arrow to move forward one song in the queue.

E. Tap the Now Playing icon to view all your songs in the queue.

7. Press Menu and note the options.

- -

WHY DO I SEE ONLY ONE MUSIC ICON FOR AN ARTIST EVEN THOUGH THERE'S MORE THAN ONE SONG FOR THAT ARTIST IN THE QUEUE? If you have more than one song from the same artist in the queue, you see only one song in the Music app screen because the app assigns one Music icon to each artist. If you want to see other songs by the same artist, flick to the Music icon that has the first song by that artist, and then tap the Forward icon. The Music icon "flips" and shows the next song from the artist on the screen. You can then play this song by tapping the Play icon.

- -

To play music on the Droid Charge, follow these steps:

1. Tap Applications, scroll to the page with the Music Player icon, and then tap Music Player.

2. Tap the song you want to play in the All Tracks list, as shown in Figure 10-14. (You can also tap Now Playing at the bottom of the screen.)

3. The song page appears, as shown in Figure 10-15. Tap the album cover for more information and playback controls that appear at the bottom of the album cover:

   A. Tap the Shuffle icon to shuffle songs in the queue.

   B. Tap the Repeat icon to repeat the same song instead of moving to a different song in the queue after the song ends.

   C. The playback timeline appears below the icons.

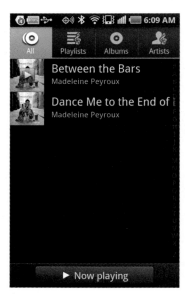

FIGURE 10-14 Tap the song you want to play in the list to open the playback page.

FIGURE 10-15 The playback screen enables you to play your song and control playback.

4. Note the playback controls below the album cover:

   A. Tap the Rewind icon to go back to the beginning of the song.

   B. Tap the Play icon to play the song. After you tap this icon, it changes to a Pause icon (two parallel lines); you can pause playback by tapping the Pause icon.

   C. Tap the Fast Forward icon to go to the next song in the queue.

   D. Tap List to return to the All Tracks list.

5. Press Menu and note the options.

Creating Playlists

As your music collection grows on your Droid, you may want to start organizing your music to make sense of it all into one or more playlists. For example, you may want to create one playlist for your favorite songs. Or you may want to create multiple playlists based on different categories such as classical music and audiobooks.

To create a playlist in the Music app on your Droid Incredible 2, follow these steps:

1. With the Music app open, tap the Library icon.

2. Tap Playlists. The Playlists screen appears, as shown in Figure 10-16.

3. Tap Add Playlist.

4. In the new Playlist screen that appears, as shown in Figure 10-17, type the name of the new playlist at the top of the screen.

5. Tap Add Songs to Playlist.

6. Select the artist who sang the songs you want to play.

7. Tap one or more songs in the list, and then tap Add.

8. Tap Save. Your new playlist appears in the Playlists screen.

9. Tap the playlist to view songs in the playlists. Tap the song to play it.

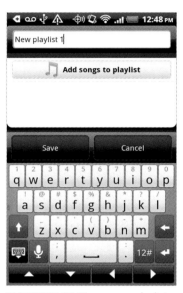

FIGURE 10-16 The Playlists screen shows all your playlists and enables you to add a new playlist.

FIGURE 10-17 Type a new playlist name and then add a new playlist.

To create a playlist in the Music Player on your Droid Charge, follow these steps:

1. With the Music Player open, tap Playlists.

2. Press Menu, and then tap Create.

3. Tap the name of the new playlist at the top of the screen, and then tap Save.

4. Tap Add Music.

5. Tap one or more songs you want to add to the playlist (or tap Select All) and then tap Add. See Figure 10-18.

6. The songs appear on your playlist page.

7. Tap the song in the playlist to play it.

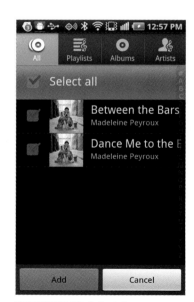

FIGURE 10-18 Select the songs you want to add to your playlist, and then tap Add.

If you want playlists of music on your Droid X2 or the Droid 3, the best way to do so is to create the playlist on your computer in Windows Media Player (or using another compatible program) and then sync that playlist to your Droid. To create a playlist in the Music Player on your Droid X2 or Droid 3, follow these steps:

1. Browse to a song on your Droid X2 or Droid 3.

2. Press Menu, and tap Add to Playlist. See Figure 10-19.

3. Make a selection: Current Playlist, New, or some other option such as a playlist you've already created.

4. If you tap New, name the playlist and tap Save.

5. Repeat.

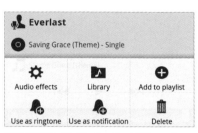

FIGURE 10-19 On the Droid X2 and Droid 3, you add songs to a playlist one at a time.

Buying Music and Media Online

If you don't have the music you want on your personal computer or home network, the Android Market offers plenty of audio and video software that you can download. You can download the app for free (or for a small price), and then you pay for the music per track or through a monthly subscription for unlimited access.

To buy music and media online, you need to access the Android Market by tapping Market on the Home screen. Following are five popular types of music and media apps and files you can download:

+ Amazon MP3

+ Android Market music files

+ Audible (for audiobooks)

+ Pandora

+ Last.fm

The benefit of all these online tools is that you can download the apps to your phone and then download the tracks directly from your phone from your home or on the go. But the apps take up additional space on your Droid's microSD card, so you need to make sure that the apps don't take up all the available storage space.

WHAT OPTIONS DO I HAVE FOR VIEWING MUSIC VIDEOS AND OTHER MEDIA? Verizon has a relationship with Blockbuster where you can download the Blockbuster app directly from the All Apps (or Applications) screen by tapping the Blockbuster icon. All four Droid models covered in this book also have the YouTube app installed. When you scroll through your apps list and tap YouTube, the app shows all recent videos on the screen. You can view music videos by pressing Settings, tapping Browse, scrolling down the category list, and then tapping Music. YouTube also categorizes music videos by most viewed, top rated, most discussed, and your top favorites.

AMAZON MP3

Amazon MP3 is a free MP3 audio file player where you can browse Amazon's online music library and pay for the tracks you want to use on your phone. Amazon MP3 is a straightforward service that enables you to browse by bestsellers, new releases, and genre. You can also search for songs, artists, and albums. The Store portion of the Amazon MP3 app is shown Figure 10-20.

   When you purchase songs you can save them onto your Droid, or you can save them on the Amazon cloud storage space at no additional charge. If you decide to use an Amazon Cloud Drive to store your music, you need to sign in using your Amazon user ID and password.

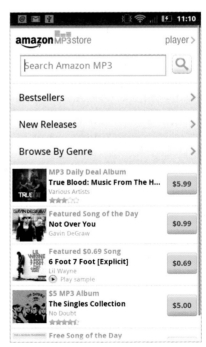

FIGURE 10-20 The Amazon MP3 Store enables you to browse in several categories and search for songs, albums, and artists.

ANDROID MARKET

The Music & Audio category in the Android Market has a lot of paid and free apps available not only for playing songs but also for creating your own songs. For example, apps like Robotic Guitarist can teach you how to play guitar.

You can also download sound files that enable you to play different sound files on your Droid. For example, if you have trouble waking, you can download a set of bugle calls used by the United States Army.

AUDIBLE

Audible is an Amazon.com subsidiary that specializes in audiobooks. The Audible for Android app is an audiobook reader that enables you to download audiobooks from your Droid and listen to them wherever you are. This app, as shown in Figure 10-21, is free and comes with excerpts from seven books, so you can get a feel for what an audiobook sounds like.

If you like the app and like the books that you hear, you can create your own account and then shop the Audible book library, with more than 85,000 titles. For a monthly fee, you can acquire credits and use them to buy audiobooks. You can also buy audiobooks with no credits at a discount. You learn more about listening to audiobooks later in this chapter.

FIGURE 10-21 You can get a feel for audiobooks by listening to a sample book in the Audible app.

PANDORA

Pandora promotes itself as providing you with a personalized radio station. After you install and run Pandora, you can add songs, artists, and composers to your "station." Then Pandora plays music in its catalog that matches what you want to play. For example, if you want to hear music by Beethoven, Pandora starts by playing a piece by Beethoven at random. Pandora will also find music related to what you've chosen, such as Bizet and Liszt for this example, and play that music at random as well.

You must create a free Pandora account to use the service. By default you can share your "station" with other Pandora users, if they're interested in listening to your music, but you can also make your profile private.

LAST.FM

Last.fm is a music-based social networking app that monitors the music you listen to on your computer, on your mobile devices, and Internet radio stations to build a profile of what you listen to. This information is posted on the user's profile page in Last.fm for other Last.fm members to see. You can also chat with other Last.fm members who have similar musical tastes.

Though membership in Last.fm is free, you must purchase a paid subscription if you want Last.fm to create your personal radio station on your phone based on your preferred artist or genre.

Listening to Audiobooks, Podcasts, and Other Audible Files

If you're old enough, you probably remember that listening to portable music started with the Sony Walkman in the late 1970s. Today you have more control over your music than ever before, but you may be surprised to know that producing audio files on a home (or work) computer has dropped to a point in which it's easy for people to record different types of audio and post it on the web and in programs that enable you post and share different types of audio files that include the following:

+ Audiobooks in which people recite the text in your favorite book.

+ Podcasts that resemble radio broadcasts, interviews, and audio lectures about different topics. Some podcasts are more like radio broadcasts (such as Rhapsody's Radio feature) and others are more freeform (such as speaking and music) and are usually produced by the narrator.

+ Other audio files, such as sound effects for your computer.

For most audio files you can use the Music app to play them. However, some specific audio file formats require a third-party app to play. The Audible app discussed earlier is one program you can use to listen to audiobooks in the Audiobook format.

USING THE MUSIC APP

Audio files come in many common audio file formats that the Music app can play, so you don't need to worry about finding a specific player. To use the music app to open an audio file, follow these steps:

1. Go to a website that contains an audible file and then download it.

2. Press Home and then tap Music.

3. Flick the Music icons to the right to view the podcast in the Music screen, as shown in Figure 10-22.

4. Tap the Play button to play the podcast.

FIGURE 10-22 The Music icons represent a different audio file. Flick the icon on top to move between different audio files and view your podcast.

CAN I SHUFFLE BETWEEN DIFFERENT PODCASTS? You certainly can shuffle between podcasts and other audio files in the Music player if you prefer not to know what you'll listen to next. Simply press Menu, tap More, and then tap Shuffle On/Off. You can also tap Repeat if you want to start playing your selected audio file again immediately after it ends.

Taking, Saving, and Sharing Video

Your Droid is not only great for playing music, but it's also a full-fledged media center. That is, your camera not only enables you to take photos to share with your network, your camera also functions as a camcorder so that you can save and share video as well, and view video on your Droid on a much larger screen (and sound system).

There are plenty of built-in controls in your camcorder including the ability to focus, zoom, flash, stabilize, and more. Though the camcorder cannot take the place of the larger, blockier camcorder that you hold in your hand, it's great for taking quick videos of what you're up to while you're on the go. When you finish taking your video, you can preview it and determine whether to save or delete it just as you would with a regular camcorder. Unlike a camcorder, the Droid's built-in connectivity features enable you to share a video via your Wi-Fi connection.

ACCESSING THE VIDEO CAMERA

The video camera, which Android refers to as the camcorder, is easy to access. In the Droid X2, Droid 3, and Droid Incredible 2, tap All Apps, and then tap Camcorder. When you open the Camcorder app for the first time in these three Droid models, the view on the video screen changes to show you what the camera sees as you move it around.

In the Droid Charge, the camcorder is not a separate application. Instead, it's included in the Camera application, so all you need to do is tap Applications and then tap Camera. Access the camcorder by tapping the Camera icon at the upper-right corner of the screen, as shown in Figure 10-23.

FIGURE 10-23 Tap the Camera icon to switch to camcorder mode.

TAKING A VIDEO

You can begin taking a video by tapping the red Record button. Figure 10-24 shows how this button appears on the Droid 3. Also notice the option to quickly switch to the digital camera. The Droid X2 does not offer this as a feature. The video timer starts and continues to run as you take the video, but this timer is not part of the video when you play it.

FIGURE 10-24 Start recording your video by tapping the red Record button.

The settings on the video and how you open the Settings menu depend on your Droid model. For example, the Settings menu on the Droid Charge is on the left side of the screen, but on the Droid Incredible 2 you need to press Menu to access the menu. On the Droid X2 and the Droid 3, press Menu, and tap Settings or another option if available. You see some or all the following settings on your Droid:

+ Switch the camera between the front and back cameras.

+ Set recording mode to normal or limit recording capabilities (such as resolution and file size) for sending via IM.

+ Set image adjustments including exposure, contrast, saturation, and sharpness.

- Set the video timer to a specific time before the camcorder starts recording.
- Change the video recording resolution.
- Select the white balance to show the white levels in the video as daylight, cloudy, incandescent, or fluorescent. The default selection is Auto.
- Add effects including grayscale, negative, sepia, and posterize.
- Change the video quality; the default is Superfine.
- Change the video review duration.
- Record the video with audio cues and include a shutter sound when you take the video.

Stop the video by tapping the Record button. The video plays for you in the recorder when you tap the Play button, as shown in Figure 10-25.

FIGURE 10-25   Tap the Play button to start playing the video you just recorded.

SAVING OR DELETING THE VIDEO

After you look at the video, you have the option to delete it. If you don't, the Droid automatically saves the video to your microSD card. You can delete a video after viewing the video, but the method depends on your Droid model.

If you have a Droid 2, Droid X3, or Droid Incredible 2, you need to delete the file from the Gallery. Follow these steps:

1. Tap Apps.

2. Tap Gallery. You may need to scroll down in the All Apps list to see the Gallery icon.

3. Tap All Videos in the Albums list. On the Droid X2 and the Droid 3, tap Camera Roll.

4. Tap the Trash icon, as shown in Figure 10-26. On the Droid X2 and the Droid 3, tap and hold the video, and then choose Delete.

5. Tap the video you want to delete, and then tap Delete. The video is removed from the thumbnail list.

FIGURE 10-26 Tap the Trash icon, and then tap the video you want to delete.

If you have a Droid Charge, to delete a video you just took, follow these steps:

1. Tap the Thumbnail icon of the video you just took below the Record button.

2. Tap the bottom of the screen.

3. Tap Delete, as shown in Figure 10-27.

FIGURE 10-27 Tap Delete in the menu to delete the video you just took.

IMMEDIATELY SHARING A VIDEO

If you like what you see from the video you just took and you want to share it with others, it's easy to do that. You learn more about sharing videos but for now consider the basics.

As with deleting a video, the type of Droid you have determines how you can share a video. On the Droid X2, Droid 3, and Droid Incredible 2, you can share videos using the Gallery.

1. Tap Apps.

2. Tap Gallery. You may need to scroll down in the All Apps list to see the Gallery icon.

3. On the Droid X2 and the Droid 3, tap Camera Roll. On the Incredible 2 and Charge, tap All Videos in the Albums list.

4. On the Droid X2 and the Droid 3, tap the video. Tap again to play it. Otherwise, tap the Share icon, as shown in Figure 10-28.

5. Review the sharing types. When you select one, tap the sharing type, and then follow the prompts to share your video.

FIGURE 10-28 Share videos with others by tapping the Share icon at the bottom of the screen.

To share the video you just took on the Droid Charge, follow these steps:

1. Below the Record button, tap the Thumbnail icon of the video you just took.

2. Tap the bottom of the screen.

3. Tap Share.

4. Review the sharing types, as shown in Figure 10-29. When you select one, tap the sharing type, and then follow the prompts to share your video.

FIGURE 10-29 Review the sharing options in the Share Video Via menu.

Using the Video and Gallery App

After you finish taking a video using your Droid camcorder, you may want to take a look at it before you post it online. Or you may have taken a video earlier, and you want to look at it again. The Video app (called Video Player on the Droid Charge) is your "clearing house" for reviewing and lightly editing videos. On the Droid X2 and the Droid 3, you use the Gallery app.

When you open the Video app in Droid Incredible 2, notice that it looks similar to the Gallery app. Indeed, you can access other Gallery items such as photos from the Video app as well. The Video Player app on the Droid Charge looks different from its Gallery app; although, when you play the video, the interface is exactly the same as it is when you play a video in the Gallery app. Of course, you're already familiar with the Gallery app on your Droid X2 and Droid 3, which you learned about in Chapter 9 ("How Do I Best Take, View, Share, and Manage Photos?").

BROWSING FOLDERS

On the Droid Charge, you don't need to worry about searching for your videos because they're all in the default Camera folder in the Videos app. On the Droid Incredible 2, browsing folders is similar to doing so in the Gallery app.

On the Droid X2 and Droid 3, you use the Gallery's Camera Roll folder. You're already familiar with how to browse those folders.

1. Tap Apps, scroll down in the All Apps list, and then tap Videos.

2. In the All Videos screen, tap the Albums icon, as shown in Figure 10-30.

3. Change to a different album by tapping a different album name in the list.

FIGURE 10-30 Tap the Albums icon to view the list of album folders.

HOW DO I ADD MORE FOLDERS FOR VIDEOS? You can add more folders by connecting your Droid to your PC or laptop with your USB cable and then setting the USB connection type to Disk Drive (on the Incredible 2 and Charge) and USB Mass Storage on the X2 and Droid 3. Your computer sees your Droid as another hard drive, so you can go into your computer's file explorer, browse to the directory that contains your videos (for example, /DCIM/100MEDIA/), create one or more new folders, and move one or more video files to the new folders.

SET AS FAVORITE

The Droid Incredible 2 enables you to select a video as your favorite in the Videos app. On the Droid X2 and the Droid 3, you can opt to add a video to an "album" and create a new album you name **Favorites** to obtain the same end result using the Gallery app. (Sorry, Droid Charge owners, but this option doesn't exist on your device.) After you set a video as a favorite or place it in an album named Favorites that you create, you can easily access those favorite videos.

To set a video as a favorite on the Droid Incredible 2, follow these steps:

1. Tap Apps, scroll down in the All Apps list, and tap Videos.

2. Tap All Videos in the Albums list.

3. On the All Videos screen, tap and hold your finger on the video you want to set as a favorite.

4. In the menu that appears, as shown in Figure 10-31, tap Set as Favorite.

5. Tap the Album icon at the lower-left corner of the screen.

6. Your favorite video appears in the new My Favorites album, as shown in Figure 10-32.

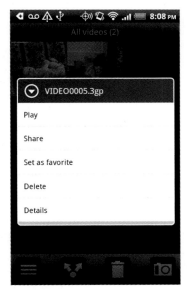

FIGURE 10-31 Tap Set as Favorite to make the video a favorite in the Albums page.

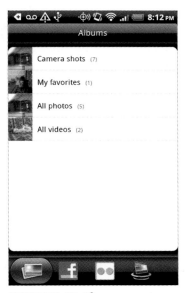

FIGURE 10-32 After you create a favorite video, it appears in the My Favorites album folder.

To add a video to a new album you create and name Favorites on the Droid X2 or Droid 3, follow these steps:

1. Open the Gallery app, tap Camera Roll, and select the video to make a favorite.

2. Press Menu on your phone, and tap Add to Album.

3. Tap New Album.

4. Name the album Favorites. See Figure 10-33.

5. Tap Save.

6. Repeat to add other videos; however, next time choose the Favorites album.

GET VIDEO DETAILS

If you need to get details about a video, such as how big it is before you decide to share it on a social networking site such as YouTube or Facebook, the Videos app or the Gallery app makes it easy to get this information. (You'll learn more about these details in the "Sharing Videos" section later in this chapter.) There are some procedural differences between Droid models.

FIGURE 10-33 Create an album on your Droid X2 or Droid 3 to hold your favorite videos.

To view details on the Droid Incredible 2, follow these steps:

1. Open the Videos or Video Player app as you did earlier in this chapter.

2. Tap and hold on the video you want information about.

3. Tap Details in the menu.

4. The details include the file path, date, size, duration, type, and status.

5. Tap OK to close the details window.

To view details in the Droid Charge, follow these steps:

1. Open the Video Player app as you did earlier in this chapter.

2. Tap Pause.

3. Press Menu.

4. Tap Details. The details list shows the filename, format, resolution, file size, and date and time the video was taken, and if the video can be forwarded. (You need to scroll down the list to see all the details.) See Figure 10-34.

FIGURE 10-34 Scroll down the list of details in the Details box to view all the details about the video.

5. Press Back to return to the video screen.

On the Droid X2 or the Droid Charge, simply tap the video once, press Menu, tap More, and tap Video Info.

DELETE A VIDEO

Sometimes you want to delete a video because there isn't enough room on the microSD card for all your videos, and you want to cull your collection. Or you may decide you want to remove the video because a newer version has taken its place. It's easy to delete an existing video on all Droid models, but the Droid Charge is a little different from the rest.

To delete a video in the Droid Charge, follow these steps:

1. Open the Video Player app as you did earlier in this chapter.

2. Press Menu.

3. Tap Remove.

4. Tap the video on the Select All screen, and then tap Remove. See Figure 10-35.

If you decide against deleting the video, tap Cancel.

To delete a video on the Droid Incredible 2, follow these steps:

1. Open the Videos app as you did earlier in this chapter.

2. Tap and hold the video thumbnail that you want to delete.

3. Tap Delete in the list, as shown in Figure 10-36. The Droid immediately deletes the video.

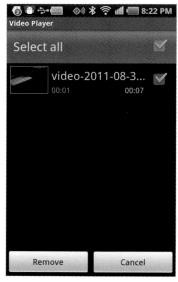

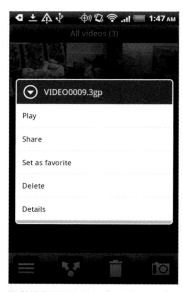

FIGURE 10-35 Tap the video in the list, and then tap Remove at the bottom of the screen to remove the video.

FIGURE 10-36 Tap the video in the list, and then tap Delete at the bottom of the list to remove the video.

If you don't want to delete the video, return to the All Vdeos screen by pressing Back.

On the Droid X2 or the Droid 3, follow these steps:

1. In Gallery, browse to the video to delete.

2. Press Menu.

3. Tap Delete.

DROID CHARGE FEATURES

The Video Player app in the Droid Charge includes some special features that the Videos app in other Droid models doesn't have. This section covers those features including bookmarks, connecting to another device via Bluetooth, and changing your video player settings.

Add, View, and Delete Bookmarks

Bookmarks in videos are similar to what you find with bookmarks for a physical book. When you add a bookmark at a specific point in the video, you can return to it by opening a list of bookmarks and tapping the bookmark to start playing the video from that point.

To add, view, and delete your bookmarks, follow these steps:

1. Open the Video Player app as you did earlier in this chapter.

2. Tap the video you want to play in the list.

3. When you reach the point in the video where you want to add the bookmark, tap Pause. You may need to move your finger up and down the playback slider to find the right point for your bookmark.

4. Press Menu.

5. Tap Add Bookmark, as shown in Figure 10-37.

6. Tap Bookmarks in the menu, as shown in Figure 10-37.

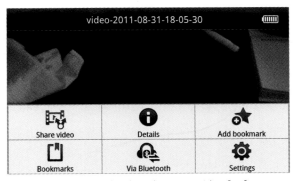

FIGURE 10-37 Add a bookmark to your video for future use by tapping Add Bookmark.

7. Your bookmarks appear in the bookmark list, as shown in Figure 10-38. The bookmark contains a thumbnail of the video at the point the bookmark was made and when the bookmark was made. For example, if the bookmark says 00:05, that means the bookmark was made 5 seconds into the video's running time.

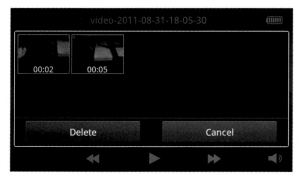

FIGURE 10-38 Tap a bookmark thumbnail to open the Play window and have the video start playing from the time specified in the bookmark title.

8. Tap the bookmark you want to use. The video begins playing from that point. If you have the video on pause, however, you need to tap Play to start playing the video.

9. Delete a bookmark by tapping Delete.

10. Tap the bookmark you want to delete, and then tap Done. See Figure 10-39.

FIGURE 10-39 Delete the selected bookmark from the list by tapping Done.

Connect via Bluetooth

When you view your videos on your phone, you may not want to call atten-
tion to yourself or be seen as rude. Therefore, the Droid Charge has an option
for you to connect the Video Player app to a set of Bluetooth-enabled headphones via the Droid Charge's Bluetooth connection. Here's how to do it:

1. Open the Video Player app as you did earlier in this chapter.

2. Open and play a video as you did earlier in this chapter.

3. Tap Pause to pause the video.

4. Press Menu.

5. Tap Via Bluetooth, as shown in Figure 10-40. The Droid scans for Bluetooth
   devices. If it finds any, follow the prompts to set up your Bluetooth device.

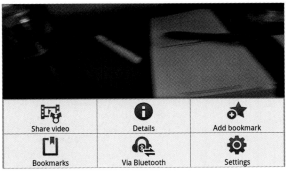

FIGURE 10-40 Tap Via Bluetooth to connect your Droid to
a Bluetooth headset to keep the sounds from the video for
your own ears.

Change Video Player Settings

When you view your video in the Video Player screen, you can change the
settings by putting the video on Pause, pressing Menu, and then tapping
Settings. You can scroll down the Settings list to view four different options:

✚ Repeat. If you want to have the video loop once or continuously loop
  when you play it, tap Repeat.

✚ Change the brightness by tapping Brightness and adjusting the brightness accordingly. If your Droid Charge is in auto-brightness mode, you
  cannot change the color level.

✦ You can change the color tone so that the video appears warmer or colder by tapping Color tone.

✦ Tap Outdoor Visibility, and turn it on if you're going to show your video outside to someone, and you need the Droid to enhance its screen capabilities so you can better see the video.

Return to the Video Player screen by pressing Back.

Editing Videos

The Droid X2 and the Droid 3 both offer options for editing the videos you take on your phone. You do that from the Gallery app, under Camera Roll, and the options become available after you tap the video you want to edit. Tap Edit to access Video Info, Tags, Trim, and Advanced Editing. Figure 10-41 shows the Trim option. You drag the end points to remove unwanted front and end matter.

FIGURE 10-41 Trim is an option on the Droid X2 and Droid 3.

You're already familiar with Video Info. Tags enables you to add "face tags" to all your images, which means you can call out people, places, and other items by typing a related keyword to denote it. This works only with images though, not videos. Additionally, Advanced Editing enables you to extract specific frames, add a title, resize the video, and remove audio.

Because what you're actually interested in here is editing the video recently recorded, focus on editing that video:

1. Open Gallery, and browse to the video to edit. Tap it.

2. Press Menu and tap Edit.

3. Tap Trim and then:

   A. As shown in Figure 10-41, drag from either end, or both, to trim the video as wanted.

   B. Press Menu, and tap Save.

   C. If wanted, type a new name and tap OK.

4. Press Menu again, tap Edit, and tap Advanced Editing; then:

   A. Press Menu once more.

   B. Tap Remove Audio if wanted, and tap Yes.

   C. Tap Add Title, if wanted, type a title name, and tap OK.

   D. Tap Resize, if wanted, and select a new size. Tap OK.

   E. Tap Extract Frame, enter a new name, and tap OK. This enables you to pull a picture from a video clip.

   F. To see the picture, return to the Gallery's Home screen, and tap My Library.

Related Questions

✦ How do I get the most from the Android Market? **PAGE 120**

✦ How do I use the Droid to communicate and work more efficiently? **ONLINE AT** www.wiley.com/go/droidcompanion

✛ INDEX